51 REASONS
WHY THE KING JAMES

A PATH FROM DOUBT TO FAITH

David W. Daniels

For a complete list of distributors near you,
call (909) 987-0771, or visit **www.chick.com**

Copyright © 2018 David W. Daniels

Published by:
CHICK PUBLICATIONS
PO Box 3500, Ontario, Calif. 91761-1019 USA
Tel: (909) 987-0771
Fax: (909) 941-8128
Web: www.chick.com
Email: postmaster@chick.com

Second Printing

Printed in the United States of America

All rights reserved. No part of this book may be reproduced, stored in a retrieval system or transmitted in any form or by any means (electronic, mechanical, photocopying, recording or otherwise) without permission in writing from the copyright owner.

ISBN: 978-0-75891-2664

Contents

Introduction 7

1 Why the KJV Says "Teach," Not
   "Make Disciples" 13

2 Why Trust a Bible That Doesn't Exist? 19

3 A Brief Word to the Critics 24

4 Why the KJV Says Cherubims and Seraphims 27

5 Modern Translations Miss the Point
   of the Nephilim 32

6 It Doesn't Matter How Far Off the Path
   You Get 42

7 Faith Is Not a Disease 45

8 Prophecy and Women's Clothing 50

9 The KJV Doesn't Add Words 55

10 We Can Trust It above Our Opinions 60

11 It Matters Which Bible You Read 65

12 Jesus' Forgiveness Matters 67

13 It Shows That God Preserved His Words Through the Flood 70

14 This Bible Is History, Not Myth 75

15 You Can Know the Line Between God's Words and Man's............................ 79

16 Muslims Can't Use It against You 83

17 "Original Autographs Only" Changes Doctrine.................................. 86

18 You Can Know What You Believe 89

19 You Can Learn from the True Church Fathers ... 91

20 It Gets Death and Hell Right 93

21 It Destroys What the Devil Wants 97

22 The Text Critics Have to Change History to Reject It 102

23 Publishers Plant Doubt to Make More Money.. 111

24 It Doesn't Let You "Have it Your Way"......... 115

25 Doubt: The Fruit of Textual Criticism 118

26 It Doesn't Need "Fixing" 121

27 Even the Devil Had to Use God's Exact Words 122

28 Your Reliable Source for Controversial
   Questions....................................125

29 The KJV Is Easier to Understand Than
   You Think....................................131

30 It Keeps Jesus Sinless 133

31 Its Doubters Aren't Sure What They Believe 137

32 It Tells You What Its Doubters Don't Want
   to Believe 140

33 A Few Tiny Changes Make a Big Difference....143

34 It Destroys Inaccurate Bible Memes...........147

35 The OAO Doctrine Was Created to Reject It ...150

36 It Exposes Confused Teachers.................156

37 It Carries the Same Inspiration as
   the Originals 158

38 It Exposes the Real Know-It-Alls.............165

39 It's a Source of Godly Zeal...................168

40 It "Reveals" the Most Changed New
   Testament Book 175

41 One Greek Letter Can Change the Gospel.....177

42 Was Jesus God on Earth? NIVs Don't Seem
   to Think So..................................182

43 It Helps You Ask the Right Questions.........189

44 It's Nothing to be Ashamed Of 192

45 It Makes It Easy to Share Your Faith 194

46 It Doesn't Need Updating 199

47 KJV Vocabulary Is Easier Than You Think 202

48 What Publishers Are Hiding.................. 204

49 What About My Congregation? 206

50 You Can Be Just Like the 90% —Or............ 209

51 Just One More Question 211

Appendix: Getting Bible Facts Straight 214

Introduction

For three nights I slept on top of my roof, over the 12x16 foot squatter's shack in the desert. The Lord had brought me back to Himself in a miraculous way, and now I had lots of questions.

* * *

Three nights before, self-centered, 17-year-old me had called down lightning from heaven —and it happened!

"I am a prophet of God!" I exclaimed.

Then I heard a voice. What I heard turned out to be an exact quote of Matthew 7:21-23 from the King James Bible:

> "Not every one that saith unto me, Lord, Lord, shall enter into the kingdom of heaven; but he that doeth the will of my Father which is in heaven. Many will say to me in that day, Lord, Lord, have we not prophesied in thy name? and in thy name have cast out devils? and in thy name done many wonderful works? And then will I profess unto them, I never knew you: depart from me, ye that work iniquity."

Those words pierced my soul. Many thoughts passed through my mind in an instant. "My Father" —that meant it had to be His Son —Jesus! But if Jesus was saying that I wasn't following Him, who *was* I following?

Then I realized there had to be a Devil, after all. All the teaching I had absorbed about taking on the "Christ-self" came tumbling down in an instant. All the occultic books I had read crumbled to nothingness.

And my thoughts went back 8 years. I had a mental picture

of that naked guy in front of the giant screen that said, "This Was Your Life!" That was the tract I read before I asked Jesus to be my Saviour.

In that moment, one thought rose to the top: "Where is my Bible?"

I scrambled down from the roof to get my huge Family Tree King James Bible. I searched until I found the words. As I read them in red letters, I thought, "God is on my roof!"

I've told about that night elsewhere, but to make a long story short, the Lord gave me my first Bible study. Afterward, I decided to stay up on the roof and read the Bible, begging God to help me find and highlight those verses. That was the first night.

The second night, I put my bedroll back up on the roof, and I started praying and asking God questions. That continued through the third night, as well.

I prayed: "Lord, I was told that people got together in a committee meeting and decided what they wanted in the Bible and out of the Bible. But God, I believe that You are big enough to superintend the scriptures, so that what You wanted in is in, and what You wanted out is out."

That was the statement of faith of a newly-repentant 17-year-old believer.

Within months, however, my King James was set aside, as a "better" New American Standard Bible was given to me as a baptismal present. Then as I prepared for Bible college, I was introduced to the Ryrie Study Bible and all sorts of other translations vying for the #1 spot.

Within a year, faith had been replaced with questions and doubt. Not doubt in God, but doubt as to what the scriptures actually said. It didn't take long. All my professors had to say was, "*God's word is inerrant in the Original Autographs. But alas, we do not have them. Still, we can be assured that **they were** inspired by God.*"

Thankfully, my faith in God was not based upon the words of my teachers. Still, what did God actually say, and could I know it?

To make a second long story short, 18 years later, I had come to find out after piles of research, that the faith I had on the roof in the desert, with nothing but God, Chick tracts and a King James Bible, was more accurate than years of studying and reading scholarly research.

Can we know that God preserved His words? **Yes!** *God promised it, so we **know** God delivered it, because God keeps His promises!*

> "...yea, let God be true, but every man a liar; as it is written, That thou mightest be justified in thy sayings, and mightest overcome when thou art judged." (Romans 3:4)

And yet, for over 200 years, modern scholars have been doing just that: judging God and His words.

How can we know God preserved His words? It's simple. First, as I said, He promised to do it.

Second, God holds us responsible for adding to or taking away from His words. It doesn't take a genius to know that we need to **have** God's words. Otherwise, how would we know whether we are adding to or taking away from them?

So, God promised to preserve His words, and to hold us accountable for changing them in any way. That means first, they exist. And second, that means we can find them.

Can you imagine what it means to **know** you have the words of God? People have climbed mountains, sought gurus, taken drugs, read libraries, even delved into the occult —just to find out what God said. And yet, God promised

His words would not be far from us. Today, they are more accessible than ever.

Now that we have mass-publishing, mass-copying, and mass-distribution, and not single, hand-copied books, we can see how essential it was that God had a plan to preserve His words. Books were spreading over the whole world. They needed to be the right words.

And God made ***Himself*** responsible for preserving them. That means He could use any person or any process He wanted to get the job done. And guess what? He did.

He used faithful, persecuted believers, for sure. The scriptures are filled with blessings for persecuted believers. But He also used faithful processes to get the job done.

When the 1500s rolled around, there was a lot of sorting of the texts that had been found. A few people prayerfully compared Bible texts, knowing that it was God's words they were collating, in order to make a single translation of the Old and New Testaments. It was a holy task.

There are a lot of stories about the different compilers. But one principle remains consistent: God was doing it through the people, whether they thought they were doing it, or not. God was keeping His promise.

God picked a man, King James VI of Scotland and I of England, to set the best scholars to their task. And it was no easy one. There were two camps: the austere, very-separate Puritans, and the ostentatious, barely post-Catholic Anglicans.

Over 54 people in total had to agree over every word of every verse of 1189 chapters of the Bible, and even throw together an uninspired Apocrypha to please the bishops. They went over every verse no less than 14 times, from 1604-1610, and then it was checked again for publication in 1611.

The result is one of the easiest things I have ever been able to gauge. People who read and believe *this Book* end up with a strong faith in God and His promises. God used those believers to bring about the largest missionary movement in history. God used this Bible to bring faith to millions. People learned to read just to devour its pages.

This book brought *hope*. People who see the faithful God in its pages have a strong expectation that the same God will keep His word to save their sinful souls and guide them into an eternity of happiness with Him.

Readers found a consistent God who never breaks His promises, even if we have no idea how He will fulfill them. We have the "hope of eternal life, which God, that cannot lie, promised before the world began" (Titus 1:2).

But starting in the 1800s, a huge, concerted effort began to bring the world under the wing of a *different* group of scholars, one approved of by Rome, who had a *different* set of Greek texts to foist upon the masses.

This Bible was *different*, alright. People who read the King James Bible found **faith**. People who read the new Bibles from these *different* manuscripts only found **doubt**.

I've written extensively about the doubt caused by these manuscripts. But it is better that you see individual cases for yourself. So, for the last six years, I have been making videos filled with examples of what the new Bibles are doing to destroy faith, and what the King James Bible does to increase faith.

This is no academic pursuit. This is here and now. Can you trust God right now, or not? If He cannot preserve for you a single book that you can trust, then how can you know He can preserve your soul?

These 51 reasons for faith in the King James Bible have

been assembled for your encouragement. May God truly increase your faith in Him and in His words.

I have found that a number of the people who fight against the King James as God's preserved words do so because they have some preferences they don't want God to pronounce against, or simply because they don't want to have a singular authority in their life.

They want a PAC Bible: a Pick-And-Choose version, with options at every turn, so they can worm out of any sin or find agreement with any religion, and have no absolute standard to judge them.

For those of us who trust God's preserved word, we can rest assured that we will know when we have followed God, and when we have not. And we will know for sure what God did say, and what He did not say.

Those who believe that the King James Bible is a literal preservation of what God spoke to His prophets and apostles will find in the following pages many reasons for their faith. A comparison of some of these reasons with the different readings in the modern versions illustrates the confusion that faces those who try to place their trust in them.

This is only a small collection of those reasons assembled from the dozens of videos I have posted to my YouTube channel. Serious consideration of only a few of these will illustrate how destructive the modern Bibles are to faith.

It will also illustrate why it is important to have a preserved standard of God's words. Otherwise, gradual changes over time will so corrupt the text that it will fit neatly into the globalist goal of one world Bible for the one world religion of the End Times.

1

Why the KJV Says "Teach," Not "Make Disciples"

Are you, or were you, a Bible college student? If so, was *your* experience in Bible college like my own? When I came to Bible college, I wanted to serve my Lord 24/7 —24 hours a day, 7 days a week. Just like I still do now. I am so totally blessed.

Anyway, when I came to Bible college in February 1981, Pacific Christian College was all about one goal. And right away in class, they stated that goal: to equip disciples to become servant-leaders. It was talked about everywhere and even painted on a central wall.

One of the scriptures they focused on was the Great Commission found in Matthew 28:18-20. Here it is, the right way, in the King James Bible:

> "And Jesus came and spake unto them, saying, All power is given unto me in heaven and in earth. Go ye therefore, and teach all nations, baptizing them in the name of the Father, and of the Son, and of the Holy Ghost: Teaching them to observe all things whatsoever I have commanded you: and, lo, I am with you alway, even unto the end of the world. Amen."

My teachers said, "In the *original Greek* it doesn't say "Go." It says, "Going," as in "While you are going..." Then they said that the next words should be translated, "make disciples of all nations," not "teach all nations." They taught us that the King James word "teach" was wrong.

They said that the King James Bible was an alright translation for *those days*, but now in the light of *modern scientific research*, that translation just doesn't measure up. But they didn't stop there. Over time they ridiculed the King James, even when I checked and one or more of their favorite versions said the very same thing!

Somehow only the King James was to blame. The others were just "alternate readings."

What was going on here? My teachers said that all translations are 99 2/3% the same, and yet somehow the King James was simply awful, horrible, no good, very bad, and something no one should read in this day and age.

Did *you* have the same experience I had? And if not in Bible college, maybe in your study group or even in a church service? It's pretty common.

But now let me answer the question: should the King James have said what the modern Greek scholars and Bibles say? Or are *its* words actually correct?

Full disclosure: I was a top student in New Testament Greek in Bible college, and I passed straight into advanced Greek at Fuller Seminary. In addition, I studied Linguistics with SIL-Wycliffe and have continued studying manuscripts of various kinds right up to today. I'm not ignorant about the Greek.

Our advanced Greek course at Fuller was focused on seeing how people will teach a rule of Greek, but then they

Why the KJV Says "Teach," Not "Make Disciples"

will quickly break it, whenever the scripture gets in the way of their personal theology.

For instance, we went over Matthew 28:19. The truth is, you don't simply translate a Greek participle by adding an "-ing" to a verb. When you do that in English, that can wrongly change the meaning of a word, or even an entire doctrine, like in 1 Corinthians 1:18.

There's a reason why it says "Go" in the King James —and most Bibles. It's because that big Greek word, πορευθέντες (*poreuthentes*), in the context simply means "Go".[1] But what about "make disciples"? Why do modern versions change it from the King James word "teach"? Let's think this one through. How do you *make* someone a disciple? If a disciple is a student, a "learner," how do you *make* him or her learn?

You've heard the old saying, "You can lead a horse to water, but you can't make him drink." Well, you can lead a student to your classroom, but you can't make him *think*, either.

But there are things we can do. That's where how we teach comes in. With a horse, we can offer it salt. If the horse licks the salt, it will become thirsty and want the water. Then he'll probably drink. Problem solved.

If I teach well enough, and excite the student with the right questions, he or she might actually *want* to learn.

The command, "make disciples" misses the whole point. God told us to teach and preach. (See Matthew 24:14; Mark 16:15; Luke 24:47; Acts 5:42 and 2 Timothy 4:2.) That is our responsibility. We are *not* in charge of their response. That's *their* responsibility.

---

1) As my son pointed out, "The same Greek word, context, and translation can be found from the same author in Matthew 2:8. Check any modern English translation!"

We cannot *make* disciples, any more than we can *make* people saved. It's an impossible task for any human being.

But we can *teach*. And we can *preach* the word, providing them with God's offer of forgiveness of their sins and eternal life, if they will trust the shed blood of His Son, the Lord Jesus Christ, to pay for their sins.

Again, *that* is our responsibility. And translations —and teachings— that change those words are simply *irresponsible*. You know what the last 36 years of study have shown me? They've shown me how the words were *already* translated correctly in English in the King James Bible.

We are to go, teach all nations, baptizing them and —here's what to teach, from verse 20: "Teaching them to *observe all things whatsoever I have commanded you.*"

How do we do that? Take another Greek class? Praise God, no! We have the scriptures!

BUT: the modern professors will tell us the scriptures are *not enough!* No —we have to trust *a man* to tell us what God **really** said. And you know how they do it? They tell you, "You cannot understand the Bible until you know the *original Greek*."

Sometimes even preachers do this. They say you must learn the ancient holy "original Greek"! Then that will unlock the *true* secrets of God in the Bible. You, too, can know "the holy language of the ancients." You too, can become a **priest** to your people! You know why? Because then you'll feel able to "correct the Bible," just like *they* do.

The truth is, people who spend their time "correcting the Bible" have little time to *learn* the Bible. And why would they? They don't believe the Bible! They believe only the sacred secrets of the "original Greek"!

They tell you the King James *English* words —of *our own*

language—are too hard. Then they push us to learn a 2,000-year-old mostly dead language, Koine Greek, as if that's simpler?

It's like someone who studies the Greek now has a special magic, just like Catholic priests who learned Latin.

But let's go back to the "go" and "teach." Where did this "going" and "make disciples" come from? Not from the 1300s through the Reformation:

> Wycliffe, 1380s: "Therfor go ye, and teche alle folkis"
>
> Tyndale, 1534: "Go therfore and teache all nacions"
>
> Cranmer, 1539: "Go ye therfore, and teach all nacions"
>
> Geneva, 1557: "Go therefore, & teach all nations"
>
> Bishops, 1568: "Go ye therfore, & teache all nations"
>
> King James, 1611: "Go ye therefore, and teach all nations"

The Jesuits also had "teach" but introduced "going" in the Rheims 1582 New Testament: "Going therfore teach ye al nations"

And guess what? It was (surprise, surprise!) Westcott and Hort in the 1881 Revised Version that introduced: "Go ye therefore, and *make disciples* of all the nations"

God told us to teach. And we can only teach *what we know; no more than we know; after we know it.*

Don't go to the Greek to try to dig for nuggets. God placed them in His preserved words, for all to see.

There are two verses that tell you what to do with the words of God. And both were changed by modern scholars. Here they are in the King James:

"Search the scriptures;" (John 5:39)

"Study to shew thyself approved unto God, a workman that needeth not to be ashamed, rightly dividing the word of truth." (2 Timothy 2:15)

Search and study. Then you can go and teach.
But that can *only* happen if you have a *Bible* you can *believe*.

2

Why Trust a Bible That Doesn't Exist?

Have you looked at your church's statement of faith lately? Is it possible it confesses faith in a Bible that does not, and never did, exist? Do you know what the "Original Autographs" are?

As I said in ***Did the Catholic Church Give Us the Bible***, the first time a person writes something down, that is called an "original autograph." So, when Moses came down from the mount, he had two stone tablets of the Ten Commandments written with the finger of God. That was an original autograph.

What happened to them? Moses got angry and he cast them at the foot of the mount and broke them to pieces. The original autograph of the 10 Commandments is gone. It's dust.

Afterward, God had Moses cut out two new tablets because he broke the ones that God gave him. And on them God wrote the first *copy* of the Ten Commandments.[2] Then those got put inside the Ark of the Covenant.

Wherever the Ark of the Covenant is, that's where the Ten Commandments are. And nobody I know is sure where the Ark of the Covenant is.

---

[2] See Exodus chapter 34 and Deuteronomy chapter 10.

So, let's face it. For all intents and purposes, the first *copy* of the Ten Commandments is gone, as well. And it doesn't matter if you call it a "2nd autograph" or the "1st copy." It's still gone. Then what happened?

God worked with Moses and, by the Holy Spirit and God's hand on his hand, gave Moses a lot of other things to write. And five books, as we know them, were made into something called a Torah Scroll, a giant scroll made of leather —animal skins.

And what happened to that? Well, believe it or not, that was placed with the Ark of the Covenant. So wherever the Ark of the Covenant is, that may be where the Torah Scroll is. What happened to it? Nobody knows.

The Levite priests would, from time to time, make copies of the original Torah Scroll of Moses or assist kings in making their required copy of the word of God, as well.

So, what did God do next? Well, God spoke to a lot of prophets and they wrote down many other books. We have Joshua through Malachi. Where are the original autographs of Joshua through Malachi? They're gone, as well.

Let's take Jeremiah. In chapter 36, God spoke to Jeremiah and he wrote down several prophecies. And they were given to not-so-good King Jehoiakim. What did he do with that manuscript?

Well, he read two or three leaves, took out his penknife, cut it into pieces and threw it in the fire. That's what happened to the original autograph of that part of Jeremiah.

Then God spoke to Jeremiah to get Baruch. And he dictated to Baruch (because Jeremiah was in prison) the same prophecies again, plus other prophecies that God gave him in the meantime.

But those same prophecies that Baruch wrote down again, that's still a copy, because the original autograph was burnt in the fire.

Then what happened? Well, if you go to Jeremiah 51, you'll see that God gave several prophecies about the future, the fate of Babylon. Then God had Jeremiah take these written prophecies and give them to Seraiah.

Seraiah, when he got to Babylon, was to open the scroll, read the prophecies, bind them up to a stone and throw it into the Euphrates River. Another original autograph gone.

Do we detect a pattern here? Is God concerned with "original autographs"? Or is God concerned with preserving His words in copies? In 2 Timothy 3:15-17 we read:

> "And that from a child thou (Timothy) hast known the holy scriptures, which are able to make thee wise unto salvation through faith which is in Christ Jesus. All scripture is given by inspiration of God, and is profitable for doctrine, for reproof, for correction, for instruction in righteousness: That the man of God may be perfect, throughly furnished unto all good works."

Timothy had no "original autographs." All Timothy had was a copy of a copy of a copy... and so on down. But that copy of a copy of a copy, God called "the holy scriptures"!

As I've shown in video after video and article after article and in numerous books, God promised to preserve His words. So why do so many "Statements of Faith" say: "We believe the Bible to be the word of God, but it's only inerrant in the autographs."

Who cares about the original autographs? All we have are copies of copies of copies. Nobody has the original autographs.

Nobody ever combined the stones that are in the Ark of the Covenant, and the Torah Scroll in animal skins, and other prophecies in animal skins, and the papyri of the New Testament together into one Original Autograph Bible. There's never been one. There isn't one. There never will be one. God never intended for there to be one. But don't despair. God promised to preserve His words:

"Heaven and earth shall pass away, but my words shall not pass away." (Matthew 24:35)

"Thou shalt keep them, O LORD, thou shalt preserve them from this generation for ever." (Psalm 12:7)

"Thy word is true from the beginning: and every one of thy righteous judgments endureth for ever." (Psalm 119:160)

God takes it upon Himself to preserve His holy words. So, all we have to do is find where they are. Now since God gives us His promise, and He preserves His words in copies, then you must believe a copy.

Brothers and sisters, I refuse to believe men. I believe God. I believe God made and kept His promise to preserve His words. There is only one Bible, copied and translated accurately for us in the English language, that passes the test and that has passed down that same inspiration: the King James Bible. I can call it SCRIPTURE without any qualification. This is the scripture in English.

Now if your statement of faith for your church says they only believe in the inspiration of God's infallible whatever, in the "autographs," they must admit that they've never seen a Bible like that in their lives, and they never shall.

By that definition, they have never seen a true Bible before, nor could they ever. They can never hold a Bible in their hands and say, "This is the preserved words of God in my language. This is the scripture." If they pretend they can, they are lying to themselves, and to everyone else.

So, if you only trust in "original autographs" that don't exist, then you doubt everything, and have faith in nothing. How can you trust what you are reading as the Bible?

I believe in God's holy and preserved words, in English, the King James Bible. I believe I have a preserved copy and an accurate translation. I believe I have 2 Timothy 3:15 fulfilled, here in my hands; the holy, inspired scripture, the King James Bible.

Go check your group's statement of faith. If they have it written like this, you may want to talk to your leaders and ask them to rewrite it. If they're serious about God's truth, they will rewrite it. Or, if they're honest, they will admit that they believe in a Bible that does not exist.

3

A Brief Word to the Critics

I once saw a brother in Christ explaining his trust of the King James Bible as his only absolute authority, and people responded with "Why should we trust him? He's not a scholar."

Wait a minute. He trusts the Bible. They trust the scholars? And he's the one with the problem?

That brought me to the question: What's so bad about trusting just one Bible? Think about it.

Let me talk to the critics for a minute. People who trust the King James Bible are getting along in life and moving forward, trusting just one Bible.

How about you? Do you have one measuring stick to gauge your Christian growth?

You see, when you spend all your time comparing versions, the one thing you're not doing is focusing on growth in obedience to Christ. It's like messing around, tuning your car engine all the time, but never actually driving anywhere.

Is it "God was manifest in the flesh," or "he appeared in a body" in 1 Timothy 3:16?

Is it "For there are three that bear record in heaven, the Father, the Word, and the Holy Ghost: and these three are one," or "for there are three that testify" in 1 John 5:7?

A Brief Word to the Critics

Should we remove the story of the woman caught in adultery, all 12 verses?[3]

Should we remove the resurrection appearances of Christ, in Mark 16:9-20?

Should we remove the need for confession of faith before baptism in Acts 8:37?

> "And Philip said, If thou believest with all thine heart, thou mayest. And he answered and said, I believe that Jesus Christ is the Son of God."

Should we remove that the gospel is "of Christ" that Paul is not ashamed of, in Romans 1:16? Does God promise to preserve and keep His words forever in Psalm 12:6-7, or did God promise to keep the Jewish people safe from their enemies forever, as in these other versions?

There are huge differences between each one of these. People who trust the King James have already made their decision which they will trust; what words they will accept, and what they will reject. And if they sit in your church, they may check whatever the preacher or teacher says, by that one holy Book. They're going to treat their King James Bible like it's —the Bible. What could be wrong with that?

From some of the remarks I've read from people on social media, I'd say they were in the seat of the scornful. We need to listen to these words:

> "Blessed is the man that walketh not in the counsel of the ungodly, nor standeth in the way of sinners, nor sitteth in the seat of the scornful. But his delight is in the law of the Lord; and in his law doth he meditate day and night." (Psalm 1:1-2)

---

3) See John 7:53-8:11

How can you meditate on the Lord's law if you cannot even settle on what it is? If the scholars cannot make up their minds, if they are scrambling after every scrap of papyrus, to find some new reading or doctrine to switch their Bible to, how can we trust them?

God tells us to "earnestly contend for the faith which was once delivered to the saints," not look under every rock or in caves in a hill for a piece of papyrus that God or an angel or a Gnostic hid there. No. It was delivered. Once. End of topic.

God keeps the truth out in the open, not hidden for scholars to find. We have a "revealed unto babes" faith, and a "hidden from the wise" faith. Jesus said it well:

> "In that hour Jesus rejoiced in spirit, and said, I thank thee, O Father, Lord of heaven and earth, that thou hast hid these things from the wise and prudent, and hast revealed them unto babes: even so, Father; for so it seemed good in thy sight. All things are delivered to me of my Father: and no man knoweth who the Son is, but the Father; and who the Father is, but the Son, and he to whom the Son will reveal him. And he turned him unto his disciples, and said privately, Blessed are the eyes which see the things that ye see: For I tell you, that many prophets and kings have desired to see those things which ye see, and have not seen them; and to hear those things which ye hear, and have not heard them." (Luke 10:21-24)

Here's the bottom line. We want to grow in faith in Christ, not stagnate in doubt. Argue if you want. Or put your trust in the 400+ year tried, tested and proved King James Bible.

What you choose is up to you.

4

Why the KJV Says Cherubims and Seraphims

If you go to Bible College or seminary, your professor may ridicule the King James, and say it's wrong when it says: "cherubims" or "seraphims." They claim it is "obvious that King James translators didn't know what they were doing."

It's popular today to say the King James Bible has made a grievous error. They have added an "s" to the ends of words that are already plural in the original Hebrew, like in Genesis 3. In Hebrew, they say, the ending "-im" is used to indicate a plural, and that's all you need. You see an "-im" at the end, and you are sure it's plural. Not so fast.

There was a good reason for putting "-ims" instead of "-im" in the King James Bible. The translators wanted the people to know whether the meaning of the word in its context referred to one, or more than one. Not all English speakers know that "-im" is plural in Hebrew.

The King James translators believed they were working with God's holy words. They didn't want to leave any meaning out, when translating it into English. And they weren't the only translators with that conviction, as you will find out.

Sometimes that -im Hebrew ending is used when referring to something that the Bible views as singular, like the mountain range Abarim in Deuteronomy 32:49: "Get thee up into this mountain Abarim, unto mount Nebo..."

These mountains in the range are referred to by the Hebrew plural name Abarim, while the highest mountain is Nebo. But the verse puts it in the singular, just like we refer to "the Sierras," "the Rockies," "the Appalachians," but it is just one mountain range.

How does that work? When children draw a mountain, it often looks something like a triangle. But most mountains don't look like triangles. They more often look like one mountain, but with many peaks, or many mountains in one range.

Some say that Mount Sinai, Mount Horeb, and even Paran are different peaks on the same mountain —or part of a mountain range. So in this verse, "this mountain, Abarim," contains "mount Nebo" as one of its peaks.

But other times the "-im" ending refers to an actual plural of objects, like the angelic beings around the throne of God. To make the fact of the plural clear to English speakers, they added a simple "-s," so it said "-ims."

Look at Exodus 25:18. It says "cherubims," and we can see why. There are two of them.

Another heavenly creature is in Isaiah 6:2. Here it says "seraphims," and again we can see why. In verse 2 it says, "each one," showing there was more than one. And in verse 6 it says, "Then flew one of the seraphims unto me." The context shows in all of these that the word is clearly plural. There is more than one seraph.

Why the KJV Says Cherubims and Seraphims

But look at Genesis 3:24, the first use of the Hebrew "-im" in the English Bible:

> "So he drove out the man; and he placed at the east of the garden of Eden Cherubims, and a flaming sword which turned every way, to keep the way of the tree of life."

Did you notice? There is nothing in the verse that tells you whether there is one or more than one. In most English Bibles, it just says "cherubim." And in most pictures, only one heavenly being is drawn.

But in the King James Bible, getting the meaning across was more important than the exact Hebrew spelling. That's why they clearly marked it "cherubims." There was more than one cherub guarding the way to Eden.

People like to pretend the translators were ignorant. But actually, this was a practice that was already occurring among Bible translators. Take a look at four other translations of Genesis 3:24:

Coverdale (Great) Bible, 1540:
"...& at the east side... he set Cherubins..."

1568 Bishops Bible:
"...and at the east side ... he set Cherubins..."

1587, 1599 Geneva Bible:
"...and at the East side ... he set the Cherubims..."

1602 Reina Valera Spanish Bible:
"...y puso al Oriente... Cherubines..."

1611 to present, King James Bible:
"... at the east of the garden of Eden Cherubims..."

The same is true for Isaiah 6:2:

1540 Coverdale (Great) Bible:
"And aboute hi stode the Seraphins..."

1568 Bishops Bible:
"And about hym stoode Seraphims..."

1587, 1599 Geneva Bible:
"The Seraphims stoode vpon it..."

Reina Valera Spanish Bible, 1602:
"Y encima del estavan Seraphines..."

And of course, the King James:
"Above it stood the seraphims..."

Some people complain, as my professors did, that it was a double-plural. Why put a second plural on the word? Well, for one, it was easy to put a simple "-s," instead of writing a Hebrew explanatory footnote everywhere it occurred.

When it was read out loud, every English speaker (or Spanish, with the Valera Bible) knew whether the Hebrew word actually meant one or more than one.

And that is the same reason that they used the already-less-used, by that time, "thee," "thou," "thy," "thine," "doest," "doeth," etc., for singular, and "ye," "you," "your," "yours," etc., for the plural. Communicating accurate meaning is that important.

What is the plural of "child"? In Early English, the word "cild," was both singular and plural. No one knew which was referred to. So how did they make it plural?

In Middle English, one way of saying it was "childer." "-er" or "-re," That communicated the plural.

But another plural of "child" was "chillen." The "-en" ending made it plural. No, that wasn't Southern slang. It was correct English.

So when the common people started saying the plural of child, both got blended together, and it became child + er + en —"Children."

Children is a double-plural that everyone uses and understands. And in the same way, everybody knows that cherubims and seraphims are more than one of each.

By the way, it was my professor, Dr. Childers, who first told me about this.

We have an amazing language, English. It adapts parts of many different languages and adds them in. It just keeps getting bigger and bigger, with other languages' rules added to our own. It's like the saying I've heard: English doesn't borrow from other languages. It follows them down dark alleyways, knocks them down and searches their pockets for loose grammar.

Our King James Bible is God's preserved words. It wasn't just made for scholars. It was made for common men, women and children —or childer, or chillen.

5

Modern Translations Miss the Point of the Nephilim

A lot of people are getting very distracted with teachings about angels mating with humans and making super-humans or half-angels. In fact, some Bible translations have left the untranslated word, Nephilim, so we have to trust the experts to tell us what it means.

Is it possible that God isn't the author of this distraction? Is it possible that the Devil has something to do with this? Perhaps the Devil is trying to distract us from listening to something important that God is saying to us.

If so, what truth is Satan trying to distract us from? We can find out by answering a few simple questions.

The Bible speaks of God the Father and His only begotten Son, but the Bible also says that there are those called "the sons of God." So who are "the sons of God" in Genesis 6?

We want to know what God said. So let me show you in Genesis 6:1-2, 4-5, KJV:

> "And it came to pass, when men began to multiply on the face of the earth, and daughters were born unto them, That the sons of God saw the daughters of men that they were fair; and they took them wives of all which they chose."

Modern Translations Miss the Point of the Nephilim

> "There were giants in the earth in those days; and also after that, when the sons of God came in unto the daughters of men, and they bare children to them, the same became mighty men which were of old, men of renown. And GOD saw that the wickedness of man was great in the earth, and that every imagination of the thoughts of his heart was only evil continually."

So, there are men on the earth, and those men had daughters. The sons of God saw those daughters of men, who were fair (beautiful), and they took wives of all the daughters of men that they chose.

There were giants on the earth *in* those days and there were **also** giants on the earth *after* those days, at the time that the sons of God made babies with the daughters of men. Those were the mighty men which were of old, men of renown. After that, the earth became so wicked that only Noah was found righteous on the earth. That's in verses 8-9.

There are five basic questions we can get from the text:

1. Who were the men?

2. Who were the daughters of those men?

3. Who were the sons of God?

4. Who were the giants (Hebrew, Nephilim)?

5. Were the giants or Nephilim the same as the babies that the sons of God had with the daughters of men?

Walk through this with me —slowly. Who or what will you trust to tell you the answers? If you already believe that angels mated with humans, surprise! There are some Bible version paraphrases made just for you! They literally wrote it into the text!

Let's start with the 2002 Message Bible. (In the video about Baphomet, I already showed its occultic leanings in the Lord's Prayer in Matthew.) This is Genesis 6, verses 1-2 and 4:

> "When the human race began to increase, with more and more daughters being born, the sons of God noticed that the daughters of men were beautiful. They looked them over and picked out wives for themselves."

> "This was back in the days (and also later) when there were giants in the land. The giants came from the union of the sons of God and the daughters of men. These were the mighty men of ancient lore, the famous ones."

So this is The Message of Eugene Peterson of 2002:

1. The *men* are the human race.

2. The *daughters* of those men are daughters of the human race.

3. The *sons of God* don't seem to be the human race, but it doesn't say.

4. The *Nephilim* are giants, like in the King James.

5. The *giants* are those babies that sons of God had with the daughters of the human race.

And after this, in verse 5 it says that "God saw that human evil was out of control."

Eugene Peterson's Message is that sons of God had giant babies with the daughters of the human race. That's one paraphrase.

The Voice Bible of 2012 goes further than Peterson, drawing a distinction between the "human" beings and the "sons of God."

Now let's look at The Common English Bible of 2011. Genesis 6, verses 1, 2 and 4:

> "When the number of people started to increase throughout the fertile land, daughters were born to them. The divine beings saw how beautiful these human women were, so they married the ones they chose."

> "In those days, giants lived on the earth and also afterward, when divine beings and human daughters had sexual relations and gave birth to children. These were the ancient heroes, famous men."

So, in the opinion of "120 biblical scholars from 22 faith traditions" for The Common English Bible of 2011:

1. The *men* are "people".

2. The *daughters* are "human women".

3. The *sons of God* are "divine beings".

4. The *Nephilim* are "giants," just like in the King James.

5. The *giants* are those children the "divine beings" had with the human women.

As I said, a number of other translations, like all of the New Century Version translations, from the English Version for the Deaf, the International Children's Bible and the generic New Century Version, through the 2014 Modern English Version, don't even translate the word "Nephilim."

They just literally put "Nephilim" in the text, so you have to trust some scholar to tell you what it means.

So where do the paraphrases leave us? We have an interesting story, if true.

In short, "the sons of God" or "divine beings" found pretty human wives and made babies. Those babies were giants or a "great warrior race." And after that, the whole world went wicked, except for one man who pleased God, named Noah.

They claim that somehow, the entire world went wicked, once angels picked out women and made powerful babies.

Is that the way the story goes? Are these paraphrases smarter than a 5th grader or can I ask a few simple questions that will blow this story to shreds?

One: Can angels make baby angels?

What verse in the Bible says angels can make baby angels?

If the paraphrasing translators didn't get that from the Bible, what book did they get it from?

There are three groups: believers, heathen and pagans.

Believers believe and follow God.

Heathen don't follow God.

Pagans follow other gods.

So, if they didn't get this story from the Bible, did it come from heathen or pagans?

And why would they trust heathen or pagan writings to interpret the Bible?

Two: Do angels have men's private body parts?

For angels to make baby angels, they have to have private body parts. For angels to make baby humans with women, they have to have men's private body parts.

Not only that, but angels would have to make baby angels the same way humans make baby humans. And angels would have to have physically compatible DNA.

What clear Bible verses state that angels have men's private body parts? And if it's not in the Bible, did they get it from a heathen book, or a pagan one? Why did they trust that book more than the Bible?

And wait. I thought angels were spirits, like in Psalm 104:4 and Hebrews 1:7. Hebrews 1:14 says:

> "Are they not all ministering spirits, sent forth to minister for them who shall be heirs of salvation?"

Jesus made the angels, so He should know what's true. He Himself said, in Luke 24:39, "...for a spirit hath not flesh and bones, as ye see me have."

Angels, which are spirits, don't have flesh and bones.

And I thought that angels don't marry and aren't given in marriage. Like it says of our resurrection in Mark 12:25:

> "For when they shall rise from the dead, they neither marry, nor are given in marriage; but are as the angels which are in heaven."

And there couldn't be unwed angels' babies running around. That's just silly. God ordained marriage —but evidently, only for earthly life, nowhere else. So, if angels do not make baby angels, angels do not have private parts, angels do not have human flesh, human bones or human DNA, how could they make human babies?

How could spirit beings mate with physical women and have human babies? What verse of the Bible says that? And if it's not there, what heathen or pagan book says that? And why would a Christian believe that book over the Bible?

Three: Why would God make them able to do that? Why would God make that even possible?

Now that you think about it, does the paraphrases' story even make sense? But what else could it possibly mean?

You can see that these paraphrases are untrustworthy. They leave us with a situation that makes no sense at all, as soon as we start asking questions. There are no baby angels in the Bible. God did not create angels to mate with humans or even marry, in the Bible.

We must place our faith in the verses of the Bible, not in a theory. First and foremost, we want every word that God said. We don't want a paraphrase. You just saw how man's opinions created a whole fairy tale story.

We need a literal Bible, with only what God said, nothing added, nothing taken away. Otherwise, how will we know if we have what God wanted us to know or not? People could take away what they didn't like and leave it blank or put something else in its place.

So, what *does* the Bible show?

In Genesis 4, Seth, the replacement for righteous Abel (Matthew 23:35), had a son named Enos. Genesis 4:26 says "then began men to call upon the name of the LORD."

So godly society had begun. But something happened that was so bad that by the time of the Flood there was only one righteous person left.

Satan has three weapons in his arsenal: the lust of the flesh, the lust of the eyes, and the pride of life.[4]

He keeps using them over and over again, because they work so well. That's his pattern. He repeats what works. And the Bible shows through history what the Devil did.

In Numbers 22-24 an enemy of Israel hired a diviner named Balaam to curse the people. God would only let him

---

4) Check out Genesis 3:6; Matthew 4:1-11; and 1 John 2:16

Modern Translations Miss the Point of the Nephilim

bless them. But Balaam was greedy and counseled one thing that would ruin the people: Get the Hebrew men to marry the pagan women. That's in Numbers 25 and 31:15-16.

In Deuteronomy 17:17, each future king of Israel was commanded, "Neither shall he multiply wives to himself, that his heart turn not away..." Yet Solomon, the wisest king in history, fell for it. 1 Kings 11:3 says, "and his wives turned away his heart." Do you detect a pattern here?

In Ezra 10:2-3 the Israelites who returned from their captivity in Babylon, had "taken strange wives of the people of the land." In verse 44 it says they even "had children" with them. In Nehemiah 13, a later group married pagan wives, as well. Each time the people of God did this it threatened to derail all that God was doing with them.

Even in the New Testament, 2 Corinthians says that being "unequally yoked together with unbelievers" is trying to join "righteousness with unrighteousness" and "light with darkness."[5]

God does not promote "missionary dating," much less marrying an unbeliever.

This is serious business.

Finally, Revelation 2:14 reminds us of Balaam again, saying he "cast a stumbling block before the children of Israel... to commit fornication."

There you have it. In the last book of the Bible, there are still men fornicating with pagan women, following the "doctrine" or teaching of Balaam —which has caused so many to quickly turn their hearts from the Lord.

Do you suppose that what Genesis 6 really does is give us the beginning of the very pattern that Satan used to pull

---

5) See also 1 Corinthians 6 and 7.

away the hearts of the people of God throughout the Bible?

There are no Bible verses (count them —zero!) warning us of a danger of humans cohabiting with angels. But there are many Bible verses warning us about the danger of the hearts of the men of God being turned away by the daughters of pagan men.

Not only that, there are entire chapters and stories devoted to telling us how it happened, what it did, and what had to be done about it.

Do you suppose that the Devil is using the story that "Nephilim are human-angelic hybrids of the union of fallen angels and women," to distract us from the real danger, of the hearts of God's people being turned away to follow pagan gods, by being unequally yoked with unbelieving daughters of men?

The supernatural scenario is in no clear verses of the Bible. People have to imply it, like in paraphrases, or go to pagan or heathen books, to find that story.

But the natural scenario, the real and present danger is all throughout the Bible, in plain sight. And yet Christians keep uniting with non-believers, as if missionary dating or marriage is suddenly supposed to work.

We can believe what the King James Bible, God's preserved words in English, says.

I think that God's people, the godly line descended from Seth through Enos, who called upon the name of the Lord, eventually had their hearts turned away from God. Why? Because they fell in love with the beautiful but unbelieving daughters of men, married them, and had children.

The Bible says the giants were already there. So their union can't have made the giants. That's not what the text of God's words says. But the Nephilim were giants.

And finally, if the union of godly men, sons of God, and daughters of men, unbelievers, produced great leaders, it makes sense that they could cause a wholesale defection of their followers, other sons of God, and of most of the godly community, to turn their hearts away from following God, just as you see throughout history.

That defection was so bad, that finally, there was only one man left who truly sought God. He was a righteous man who walked with God. His name was Noah. And the rest, as they say, is history.

I'm going to trust the Bible story, not the pagans' fairy tale. You can, too.

6

It Doesn't Matter How Far Off the Path You Get...

We've had it all backwards. It's just like being a teenager: "How far can I go and still be a good boy" or "a good girl"? We try to see how much compromise we can get away with, and still have people call us "faithful."

It's the same thing with the Bible version issue. People want to be "King James preferred," but not "King James only." People switch to the New King James, Modern King James, Modern English Version, King James II, III, 21st Century, Millennium, American, Easy Reading, just so it's not "only" the King James.

"It's the same text," they say, "and the same translation, mostly, sort of. And besides, it's just one or two errors in the text."

As a teenager, it's not about what you can get away with; it's about the fact that your body is no longer pure.

The Devil doesn't care how far off the King James trail you go, just as long as it's not the actual King James. You start in a slightly different direction, but eventually you end up a long way off the trail.

Today the pope is gathering people from all religions and non-religions. I have articles and quotes from the pope. He's courted just about everyone, from atheists to homosexuals, from Baptists to Buddhists, from Qur'an followers to the United Bible Societies.

What do they agree on? The amazing thing is they don't agree on anything, it seems, except one thing: they are all against the Fundamentalists, the Christians who believe they have one preserved final authority, a Book preserved through history that absolutely expresses the mind of God, and, in their language, is the words of God. For us in English, that is the King James Bible.

That's it. They agree on a common enemy. For example, even Martians are allowed into this group. On Vatican Radio, on May 12, 2014, the pope said:

> "If —for example— tomorrow an expedition of Martians came, and some of them came to us, here… Martians, right? Green, with that long nose and big ears, just like children paint them… And one says, 'But I want to be baptized!' What would happen?"

Then the pope referred to Acts 11, to what Peter said:

> "If then God gave them the same gift He gave to us when we came to believe in the Lord Jesus Christ, who was I to be able to hinder God?"

So Martians are in. But believers in the preserved Bible, whom the pope calls "ideologues" and "fundamentalists," are out.

On October 17, 2013, the pope said:

> "In ideologies there is not Jesus… And ideologies are rigid, always… But it is a serious illness, this of ideological Christians. It is an illness, but it is not new, eh?"

On November 27-29, 2013, the pope told his fellow Jesuits that being a fundamentalist "is not healthy." On June 13, 2014, he said:

> "A fundamentalist group, although it may not kill anyone, although it may not strike anyone, is violent. The mental structure of fundamentalists is violence in the name of God."

On November 30, 2014, he said:

> "You ... can't say that all Christians are fundamentalists. We have our share of them (fundamentalists). All religions have these little groups."

And that's the Devil's goal: to make preserved-Bible believing Christians as little of a group as possible. It doesn't matter which Bible you use, even a King James lookalike, as long as it's not God's preserved words, in English, the King James Bible.

If you are willing to abandon the preserved words of God for anything else, the pope has a great place for you: by his side, as his friend. But God says:

> "Ye adulterers and adulteresses, know ye not that the friendship of the world is enmity with God? whosoever therefore will be a friend of the world is the enemy of God." (James 4:4)

Which side do you want to be on?

7

Faith Is Not a Disease

People treat King James Only as if it's a disease.

But it's not a disease. It's the one thing the Christian has been hoping for: FAITH!

It is faith-producing. It is faith-encouraging. It is faith-bolstering. It is faith-increasing. It is having one resource to turn to, where you know it's 100% right. And when properly and prayerfully understood, it will never steer you wrong.

So how does it help, practically, for an English speaker to trust the King James Only?

Here are some of the ways: A brother in Christ came home from a church yesterday, frustrated. At one point in the sermon, the pastor had said, "This is a poor translation. A better translation would be..."

"According to who?!" he said to himself. Others around him turned in their seats and looked at him. He had said it a little louder than he thought!

Well, maybe that planted a seed.

If I say, "a better translation would be," I have decided to judge, not from one authority, but among many authorities. But if I am judging among the authorities which one I think is best, I am standing above the authorities, aren't I?

So, what am I trusting? My own wisdom!

I don't want to trust my own wisdom. That is why I want

God's wisdom. And to have God's wisdom I need to have God's words. Only God's words will give me God's understanding and wisdom. Only God's words have God's seal of approval on them.

It only makes sense, right?

I don't want a Jesus in my back pocket and a mess of Bibles under my feet. I don't want to stand OVER the word, to judge it. I want to stand UNDER my God, and have His words judge OVER me.

That is why I'm King James Only. I only want God's words. And only the King James Bible in English has the textual history, and the track record.

There is the King James Bible and there are the contenders who desire to take its place. But this isn't the Bible Olympics. There are no Gold, Silver and Bronze medal Bibles. There is simply the Bible, that is God's words in a given language. And there are the other ones, that are not God's words. It's as simple as that. It doesn't matter if it's 50%, 10% or 1% man's words. If it's man's words, it's no longer God's words.

So then, how can we have faith in God's words if our Bible contains a mixture of man's words and God's words? How could you know which of them is which? Trusting any of man's words would mean we have placed our trust in fallible man.

The Bible in English, the King James Bible, has been tried, tested and proved for over 400 years. It has a track record of producing in faithful, prayerful people what God says in the Bible He wants to produce: good fruit.

When I started to read one chapter of Proverbs a day (there are 31 days in the longer months, and 31 chapters in Proverbs), and did it prayerfully, it changed my life. It kept me out of some big problems.

Proverbs 6:1-5 says you must not be "surety for thy friend," or have "stricken thy hand with a stranger." Just one implication of this is "don't co-sign with anyone." Don't put yourself in the position that you pay if he or she doesn't.

That's not man's words. That's God's words. My finances were protected at a crucial time.

Proverbs 18:1 says, "Through desire a man, having separated himself, seeketh and intermeddleth with all wisdom." "Intermeddle" here means to interfere with what God says is wise.

Other Bibles don't say that, by the way. But what I learned was to watch out for people who separate from the rest for a while, and then come back, and suddenly change from wise teachings.

They change what God said in the Bible to do, according to their own desire. Then they start to claim that they have more authority than others and that they have no need of godly counselors. Sometimes they even dismiss their own elders or deacons and select "Yes-men," instead.

There are pastor-teachers like that. And more than a few cults have been started that way. They get rid of sound counsel, just like King Rehoboam dismissed Solomon's counselors for his own desires, selecting his un-wise peers. That's how Rehoboam lost the Northern Kingdom of Israel, you know. Check out 1 Kings 12 and 2 Chronicles 10.

Other Bibles say other things. But the King James says it right, and it bears out in other scriptures.

That's another point about the King James over all the others. It doesn't disagree from scripture to scripture. And if you don't understand an idea, you can check similar scriptures, to help you better understand.

We trust, have faith in, all the scriptures, so much that we know one scripture will not contradict another, any more than God can contradict Himself.

Modern versions don't have that. When you go from one verse to the next, they say different things. And their Bibles lower Christ and cause you to doubt the Godhead, angels, devils, heaven, hell and start thinking that it's works that get you saved, rather than works that were made for you to please God AFTER you have faith in Him and AFTER you are saved.

My Bible does this, and so much more. I'm just getting started.

I have one source. That one source, correctly and prayerfully understood, will never lead me wrong. That one source, I am under and not over. That one source does not leave other options open to me. If I choose to trust the King James only, it cuts both ways. I don't get it my way. I get it God's way, which IS the high way.

Trusting only the King James Bible has enabled me to question anyone who says anything contrary to it. I have a standard!

Can you imagine a group of people trying to build a building, if everyone measured a foot by his or her own foot size? No one would have the same measurement! Nothing would fit together!

That is what it's like trying to build up one another, or a pastor his congregation, with a multitude of Bibles, or even one, with a mixture of man's words with God's words. If you don't have God's one pure measurement, then how can you fit a building together the way God wants?

And it's the same when the pastor or teacher says, "a better

Faith Is Not a Disease 49

reading would be..." He has introduced a yardstick based on his own foot size! It will never measure up to what God wants.

That doesn't bring growth, brothers and sisters. It brings confusion. The four downward steps that Satan set down in the garden of Eden are in almost every Bible college and seminary, and many of the churches:

1. Confusion: "Yea, hath God said?" "Did God say it, or not? I'm not really sure what that verse says."

2. Doubt: "I'm no longer sure that that teaching is in the Bible."

3. Disbelief: "I don't think God said anything about that."

4. Rebellion: "I'm gonna just decide for myself what I like the best, and I'll go my own way."

The only step up is FAITH in God's words. I want to step up. I want to grow in faith.

But to have that, you need God's words, and only God's words. So, in English, I'm staying with the 400-plus-years tried, tested and proved King James —only. How about you?

8

Prophecy and Women's Clothing

I'd like to talk to you about two controversial things: prophecy and women's clothing.

What is prophecy?

At its base, prophecy is speaking the words of God to people. The prophet Ezekiel related these words in Ezekiel 2:3-5:

> "And he [God] said unto me, Son of man, I send thee to the children of Israel, to a rebellious nation that hath rebelled against me: they and their fathers have transgressed against me, even unto this very day. For they are impudent children and stiffhearted. I do send thee unto them; and thou shalt say unto them, Thus saith the Lord GOD. And they, whether they will hear, or whether they will forbear, (for they are a rebellious house,) yet shall know that there hath been a prophet among them."

So, a prophet is a person who gives a message from God. What kind of message is it? Verse 4, "...Thus saith the Lord GOD." Not, "This is the general meaning of what God said," or "This is a cultural substitute for what God actually meant," or "Thus saith my Bible college professor," but "This IS what the Lord actually said."

Prophecy and Women's Clothing

The prophets were confident, because they were right. They weren't speaking for themselves, but for God.

Did you know that the Bible says if everyone prophesied, it would actually be a good thing? In 1 Corinthians 14:24-25, God spoke through Paul:

> "But if all prophesy, and there come in one that believeth not, or one unlearned, he is convinced of all, he is judged of all: And thus are the secrets of his heart made manifest; and so falling down on his face he will worship God, and report that God is in you of a truth."

Why would he fall on his face and worship God? Why would he report that God is in you of a truth? Because you all spoke the words of God! That means you all spoke the same things!

Think about your church. Can you honestly say that if someone unlearned in the Bible or an unbeliever comes in, that all could take their Bibles and show the same truths about that person's life?

But if you had God's words, you could do that, couldn't you? But, really, if you had the NIV, ESV, NLT, New King James, all I can say is, "Good luck with that."

Check out a controversial pair of verses:

> "Know ye not that the unrighteous shall not inherit the kingdom of God? Be not deceived: neither fornicators, nor idolaters, nor adulterers, nor effeminate, nor abusers of themselves with mankind, Nor thieves, nor covetous, nor drunkards, nor revilers, nor extortioners, shall inherit the kingdom of God."
> (1 Corinthians 6:9-10)

Let's go back to verse 9. The 1984 NIV says that the last two are: "...nor male prostitutes nor homosexual offenders…"

It's in the 1984 NIV, but there's a huge change in the 2011 NIV! Watch carefully. In the 2011 it says, " ...nor men who have sex with men."

That's MSM in the abbreviation. What happened? Check out the footnote: It says, "The words men who have sex with men translate two Greek words that refer to the passive and active participants in homosexual acts."

By strange coincidence, those words, the MSM, are also the very words used by the Centers for Disease Control. It even has its own Wikipedia page.

The ESV says "... nor men who practice homosexuality," But it has a similar note. So do the Common English Bible, the newest change to the Holman Christian Standard (yes, they keep changing it), and the NET Bible.

The NLT has a different perspective. It says: "...or are male prostitutes, or practice homosexuality," And the New King James goes in a different direction. It says, "...nor homosexuals, nor sodomites,"

Confused yet?

Believe it or not, a number of Bible versions actually agree with the King James word "effeminate," including Westcott and Hort's ASV and ERV, the New American Standard, the Noyes, Rotherham, Webster, Revised Webster and Young's Literal.

They hadn't changed it yet, you see.

What is ***effeminate***, anyway? Webster's 1828 dictionary says it exactly: "Having the qualities of the female sex; soft or delicate to an unmanly degree; tender; womanish; voluptuous."

Prophecy and Women's Clothing

Think about it. It goes way further than male prostitute, submissive homosexual or MSM. It means a guy who acts like a girl, a man who acts like a woman. It's a man who is unmanly. That covers a lot more ground, doesn't it?

So, if you go to a church and the male worship leader is dressed in a soft shirt with a woman's sweater and women's tight pants —that's not homosexual, but it is ***effeminate***. If a guy puts on a dress and high heels, that's effeminate, too.

If a guy acts like a girl, taking on a girl's mannerisms, that may not be homosexual, but it is ***effeminate***. And God says that should not be, especially in Christians.

Homosexuality is way further down the line from ***effeminate***, but God won't allow either in His people, according to His preserved words. You see, many people, they're like Lot. They set their tent so close to the Devil's land, like Sodom, that they have to engage in a property dispute. But God says: "Don't even go there."

Now if everyone in your church had the KJV, there would be no excuse. Don't look like a woman, men. Don't look like a girl, boys. One message.

And if someone were convicted by these holy words, this one message, think about it. 1 Corinthians 14:24-25 could actually come true, in a sense:

> "But if all prophesy, and there come in one that believeth not, or one unlearned, he is convinced of all, he is judged of all:"

Why? Because they have the same words.

> "And thus are the secrets of his heart made manifest; and so falling down on his face he will worship God, and report that God is in you of a truth."

My Bible says one message: *This is God's words, written in English*. And you will only have one message if you will trust God's holy words in English, the King James Bible. It will take out all the guesswork! You will be as confident as a prophet and be able to say, "Thus saith the Lord!"

Because you will be right.

9

The KJV Doesn't Add Words

I have heard an argument by people who want to be styled as text scholars or text critics that says it's not the ancient Alexandrian intellectuals who **took away** from God's words. Instead, they say that Bible believers **added** to God's words!

How could anyone set aside the Bible of the persecuted believers, passed down even at the cost of their lives through the centuries? Remember, this was the same preserved text that God used to cause the Reformation, which saved so many Catholics and delivered them from bondage to Rome. The Devil had a solution. All the way back in the 1860s, two fellows named Westcott and Hort made up an amazing fairy tale story, to get people to put down the very Bible that saved them and all the Christians they knew.

* * *

Once upon a time in the 200s or 300s AD, all the important ministers of the world gathered together for a big meeting. They wanted to decide on one Bible text for everyone to read.[6]

Everybody had different texts, many of them with many more words than the special scholars of Alexandria had in their Bibles. The less-intelligent ministers added in words to make the Bible make more sense to them. Since God didn't make His words clear (that Jesus was eternally God, part of the Godhead, and that He was sinless and did not lie, etc.) they thought they would fix the New Testament by putting in extra words that "smoothed out" the text for them.

The committee loved all the new additions. And soon, as if with a giant photocopier, all the ministers copied down this new text and took the copies home to their churches. And that text spread far and wide, all over the world. And that, Westcott and Hort said, is why the Bible texts in what to date are 5,700 Greek manuscripts, are mostly like the King James, and only 44 are actually classed "Alexandrian."

According to Westcott and Hort, the people copied those, instead of the "truly accurate copies" that were left to sit largely unused and undiscovered in desert monasteries or the Vatican until the 19th century.

What makes this story so amazing is that it has absolutely

---

6) Some pretend this happened at the Council of Nicaea (325 AD). We have documentation of this council. Nothing in it had anything to do with determining the Bible text. The most they could point to is Jerome's preface to Judith, telling how he was *forced* to add an error-ridden version of it to his Catholic Latin Vulgate: "Among the Jews, the book of Judith is considered among the apocrypha.... But ... the Nicene Council is considered to have counted this book among the number of sacred Scriptures..." (See Jerome's preface to Judith at *www.tertullian.org*).

no historical documentation whatsoever. They just made it up out of their heads.

And what's crazier, most everyone seemed to buy it!

* * *

People who trust the King James have a different point of view. They say that unbelievers in Egypt took away from God's words, to change the Bible books to suit their own unbelief—and strange beliefs, as well.

Which point of view is correct? Let's think this through.

The Bible believers, the ones who believe they are under a curse if they add to or take away from God's words, are the very ones these text critics say added to and took away from God's words.

Take a look at Proverbs 30:5-6:

> "Every word of God is pure: he is a shield unto them that put their trust in him. Add thou not unto his words, lest he reprove thee, and thou be found a liar."

The critics say that the believers, who literally believe that God will find them a liar if they add to His words, are the very ones who added to His words.

> "Ye shall not add unto the word which I command you, neither shall ye diminish ought from it, that ye may keep the commandments of the LORD your God which I command you." (Deuteronomy 4:2)

For the text critics' and these text scholars' theory to be correct, the Bible believers, who actually believe that a literal God spoke this to a literal Moses, and who want to obey the commandments of God, actually added to and diminished from God's words, so that they can't tell which words are God's, to obey them?

Take a look at Revelation 22:19:

> "And if any man shall take away from the words of the book of this prophecy, God shall take away his part out of the book of life, and out of the holy city, and from the things which are written in this book."

Textual critics say Bible believers changed 'tree of life' in Revelation 22:19 from "eating from the tree of life" to "the book of life," And in addition, text critics say the Bible believers changed Revelation more than any other book of the Bible.

The very people who believe that they would be under a curse, put themselves under a curse by changing the words of God?

Those who want to be known as text scholars or text critics want us to believe that the ancient Alexandrians, who did not believe God's words, who spiritualized God's words, who rationalized God's words, who refused to take them literally to the point of saying they are lies intentionally put there by God, as Origen said in *De Principiis*, Book 4, sections 8-19, —those text critics are saying the Alexandrians are the only ones who cared enough to preserve God's words?

And their evidence is... what? "Ye shall know them by their fruits." (Matthew 7:16) The Bible believers have literally thousands of manuscripts that agree with one another, around the world and through time.

The text critics love the city of Alexandria. The city of Alexandria and the school of Alexandria wasn't even able to produce two manuscripts that agree.

I don't know about you, but I side with the people who are scared to death to add to or take away from God's words. I side with the people who have the evidence of thousands of manuscripts that actually agree and who believe those curses and don't want to make God unhappy.

That's why I believe my King James Bible. Nothing added. Nothing taken away. The pure words of God faithfully translated and preserved in English.

I hope you do, too.

10

We Can Trust It above Our Opinions

Do you want to see how trying to explain a Bible passage in words my kids could understand, completely changed my End Times doctrine? One day I was sitting in the living room with my three oldest sons, Michael, Matthew and John, and I had Zechariah 14 open in my Bible.

I had already come to believe that the King James Bible was God's preserved words in English. That means I didn't have any "wiggle room" to switch to another Bible version to reinterpret the text. I was only going to use the historically preserved words of God, the King James, from then on.

I was also already working with Jack at Chick Publications. And I didn't share his Premillennial, Pre-Tribulation views at all. But it was his company, not mine. (Of course, he said it was the Lord's company, but you get my point.) I wasn't in charge of the End Times views. Thank God!

You see, for 18 years I was an Amillennialist. I called it "church-age millennialism." The "thousand years" of Revelation 20 wasn't literal. It stood for the church age. The first resurrection wasn't literal. It was a symbol for salvation. And the Gentile/Jewish church completely replaced Israel. God no longer had any plans for Israel.

Now, I knew that there were a number of undeniable

verses that I totally accepted from the New Testament concerning the 2nd Coming of the Lord Jesus Christ. There was no debate about verses like these:

> "Behold, he cometh with clouds; and every eye shall see him, and they also which pierced him: and all kindreds of the earth shall wail because of him. Even so, Amen." (Revelation 1:7)

A few days after Jesus' triumphal entry into Jerusalem, Jesus said this to Jerusalem:

> "Behold, your house is left unto you desolate: and verily I say unto you, Ye shall not see me, until the time come when ye shall say, Blessed is he that cometh in the name of the Lord." (Luke 13:35)

After Jesus had been speaking:

> "And when he had spoken these things, while they beheld, he was taken up; and a cloud received him out of their sight. And while they looked stedfastly toward heaven as he went up, behold, two men stood by them in white apparel; Which also said, Ye men of Galilee, why stand ye gazing up into heaven? this same Jesus, which is taken up from you into heaven, shall so come in like manner as ye have seen him go into heaven. Then returned they unto Jerusalem from the mount called Olivet, which is from Jerusalem a sabbath day's journey." (Acts 1:9-12)

Now I was clear on a number of things from these New Testament verses:

1. Every eye shall see Jesus.
2. This includes "they that pierced Him" (which means

either He'd raise the first century people from the dead before He comes, or it is a general reference to the Jewish people).
3. At least some Jewish people of Jerusalem will say, "Blessed is he that cometh in the name of the Lord."
4. Jesus will descend from heaven onto Olivet (the Mount of Olives), in like manner as he ascended up into heaven from the Mount of Olives.

So, I wanted to show how these were going to come to pass to my three oldest kids, 12, 9 and 7. The best passage to show how this happens would be Zechariah 14, verse 4:

> "And his feet shall stand in that day upon the mount of Olives, which is before Jerusalem on the east, and the mount of Olives shall cleave in the midst thereof toward the east and toward the west, and there shall be a very great valley; and half of the mountain shall remove toward the north, and half of it toward the south."

Wow! See? Jesus will stand on the Mount of Olives! But it doesn't say "LORD" in verse 4. Where does it say "the LORD"? Back in verse 3:

> "Then shall the LORD go forth, and fight against those nations, as when he fought in the day of battle."

There's your proof. It's the Lord Jesus who will set His foot on the Mount of Olives. But who are "those nations"? I had to go back to verse 2:

> "For I will gather all nations against Jerusalem to battle; and the city shall be taken, and the houses rifled, and the women ravished; and half of the city shall go forth into captivity, and the residue of the people shall not be cut off from the city."

So, half the city of Jerusalem, the "residue of the people," must be who the Lord is defending. He's setting foot on the Mount of Olives to do something. He's splitting it east to west, then sliding half north and half south to make a "great valley."

Part of my End Times views are already being demolished in front of my boys. Jesus is focused on people in Jerusalem. He has to have a plan for Israel that is not just "the church." All nations, or Gentiles, will be gathered against Jerusalem. It's Gentiles against Jews. That didn't fit Amillennialism.

But then what happens? Why did Jesus split the Mount of Olives? Look forward to verse 5:

> "And ye shall flee to the valley of the mountains; for the valley of the mountains shall reach unto Azal: yea, ye shall flee, like as ye fled from before the earthquake in the days of Uzziah king of Judah: and the LORD my God shall come, and all the saints with thee."

Thee —that's singular. It's not the plural, "ye," like it is for the Jewish people. The only one this can be referring to is the LORD Jesus, the one who is coming. So, half a city of Jewish people shall flee through that space created by the splitting north and south of the Mount of Olives.

And did you see those last words? "and the LORD my God shall come, and all the saints with thee"!

"The Lord my God shall come" where? Jesus had already come to earth. There was only one other place mentioned: Jerusalem! But Jesus has the saints with Him, as well! It is so amazing that Zechariah the prophet turned toward God and said: "and all the saints with Thee!"

Okay. So I found there was a separate plan, at least for some Jewish people at the end. There was no denying it.

After this, there are 16 more verses in the chapter. And guess what they have to do with? Life in Jerusalem and about the nations of the world AFTER this big event!

That was a problem for me. I thought Jesus would return, and that would be it. He'd destroy the heavens and earth, then judgment day, then the new heavens and earth. No more time on this earth.

But this describes being on earth, after the second coming. It was obvious. And this related to a lot of other verses I knew.

I had read through the Bible a number of times, and kept reading it, like many do. I knew that in the 1,189 chapters of the Bible, there was only one place designating a time period after the 2nd Coming of the Lord Jesus. And that is the 1,000 years of Revelation 20, "the Millennium."

So, instantly I had become a Pre-Millennialist. Jesus would come back before a millennium. I was totally wrong for 18 years. And now the simplest of questions, in just four verses, taking my King James Bible literally, without excuses, led me there. Once I realized that a lot of the verses were literally fulfilled or described as literal in the New Testament, I realized I could no longer spiritualize all the other verses. They also had to be fulfilled, literally.

That was the beginning of how my End Times views changed.

It only takes a few carefully-read verses to sweep away unbiblical doctrines. But to do that, we don't want man's opinions. We need to have exactly what God said.

Thank God, we do.

11

It Matters Which Bible You Read

It doesn't matter which Bible you buy. It matters which Bible you read.

Would you like to know the Bible that people have been reading? Some highly reputable groups in the publishing industry have been studying Bible trends. And they found that the Bible which people buy, and the Bible people read are two different things.

Which Bible we buy is influenced by a bunch of factors:

1. What church we go to.
2. What college we attend. Many Bible colleges will tell you which Bible or Bibles are expected to be used in that school. (Master's College at least used to require people to have the ESV. Fuller Seminary used to push the New Revised Standard with Apocrypha, sometimes called Deuterocanonicals).
3. What is popular.
4. What has the latest study notes, new versions, etc.
5. And definitely, what our favorite professor, or preacher or pastor likes.

But you know what influences which Bible we read — when we actually want answers from God? That's when the rubber meets the road. According to the study, "The Bible in American Life" from Indiana University at Perdue, of people who actually read the Bible, 55% read the King James Bible. Only 19% read the NIV. And the rest are single digits: The New Revised Standard, 7%, Catholic New American Bible, 6%, Living Bible, 5%. And other translations combined, 8%.

Mark Noll, a *Christianity Today* writer and a professor at the Catholic Notre Dame University, who oversaw this study said: "Although the bookstores are now crowded with alternative versions, and although several different translations are now widely used in church services and for preaching, the large presence of the KJV testifies to the extraordinary power of this one classic English text."

People can tell you the King James is "too hard." But believe it or not, they've been saying that for centuries. You don't need me to tell you: books that are too hard go away. The King James isn't going anywhere.

The American Bible Society is no friend of the King James. And yet, even they could not ignore their own study, the "State of the Bible" report. The Barna Group did the survey for them. Their numbers said 52% of Americans read the King James or NKJV. (They're trying to group them together. But they're not really the same.) But only 11% read the NIV.

How about Google? According to the Bible Gateway's Stephen Smith: Nearly 45% of all Bible translation-related searches were King James. Almost 24% for the NIV. Plus, searches for the King James have actually been rising since 2005, where the other translations have been flat or declining.

Suddenly, the picture doesn't look the way professors and publishers have been claiming.

It doesn't matter which Bible we buy. We have lots of reasons for why we buy one. What *really* matters is which Bible we read —and believe.

12

Jesus' Forgiveness Matters

It's the most momentous event in history. The Creator of the Universe is giving Himself to be murdered by men. They are actually in the process of doing it —and jeering at him while they're doing it!

And Jesus, on the cross, forgives them!

It's so important, it's the first sentence He says from the cross! Luke 23:34, you probably know it by heart:

> "Then said Jesus, Father, forgive them; for they know not what they do…"

And then they put a footnote in that suggests maybe you should take it out of your Bible? What kind of person would do that? Wait till you find out.

This sentence, from the cross, has helped me more than once. The act of forgiving people who have wronged me, or that are wronging me, that is major stuff.

That is also one of the differences between Christianity and every religion on the face of the earth, throughout all time.

And I'm led to question it with the addition of a single footnote?

"Yea, hath God said…?"

It's insidious.

Think about this: How many Bible versions do you know of, that are missing those words?

Go ahead. Find out. Or even, get out your program: Get out BibleWorks, E-Sword, Online Bible, SwordSearcher, whatever. Oh, it's right there, isn't it?

Yes, it is.

Look up Tischendorf, Tregelles, von Soden, Westcott and Hort! They have it in the Greek text. Yes, the last two have it in brackets. But it's still there.

Alexandrinus has it. Sinaiticus had it —the first corrector took it out, then the second corrector put it back in!

And of course, Vaticanus is completely missing it. You know why those Alexandrians may have taken it out?

Jesus forgave everyone who murdered him. That includes the Jews. And some people don't like that. Some people don't like the Jewish people.

Like, say, Joseph Smith. His so-called "Inspired Version" actually added words and put them in parentheses into the verse. Yes, only he would come up with a revelation out of nowhere and add it to the text, so consider the source.

But here in Joseph Smith's "Inspired Version" it's verse 35 instead of 34. He added a whole verse into the chapter.

> "Then said Jesus, Father, forgive them; for they know not what they do. (Meaning the soldiers who crucified him,)"

Out of all the Bibles I have collected since 1980, only ONE removes Jesus' words of forgiveness, Charles B. Williams' "The New Testament: A Translation in the Language of the People," 1949, Moody Press.

Only he had the unmitigated gall to completely remove it from the Bible. I bought it for 50 cents in a Christian college library, before they threw it in the trash where it belonged. Yeah, I rescued it.

But wait. A lot of those other versions have a tiny little *footnote*. I gave the New King James over 10 years of my life. It's supposed to be an updated King James, that "preserves the majesty" of the King James language, words, —whatever.

But look at the footnote. At Luke 23:34 it says: "NU (meaning 'Nestles-UBS critical Greek Text') brackets the first sentence as a later addition."

That's what you call a "Yea, hath God said?" note. "We don't have the guts to take it out ourselves, but maybe *you* might want to."

These scholars can't take it out of their Bible, but they put a tiny, faith-destroying note to make you doubt the most magnificent, overwhelmingly wonderful gift of forgiveness, and remove it from your Bible —even in the New King James.

Shame on them. Trust your King James, God's preserved words in English, not the "New" one.

13

It Shows That God Preserved His Words Through the Flood

When I was in Bible college, and then in seminary at Fuller, I learned about "Bible scholars" of the past who said that Moses couldn't have written the Pentateuch (the first five books of the Bible, Genesis, Exodus, Leviticus, Numbers, and Deuteronomy), because writing was not invented yet!

Okay, then archaeology came in and proved *that* to be a lie! There was lots of writing in the time of Moses, all the way back to the time of Abraham.

But what about the time before that? For instance, when was Genesis written?

Another thing we heard about in seminary was something called the "Documentary Hypothesis." It went like this: basically, all of the Old Testament was written in a short period between the 800s and the 500s BC, for the most part.

No, really.

Another story I heard was that Moses actually wrote Genesis, because it came down from heaven. God revealed it to Moses while he was up on top of Mount Sinai. That comes from something called the "Oral Torah." That's Jewish tradition that was placed on an equal level with scripture.

Is that true? Well, all that really does is back up the claim that it was never written down before Moses, and that actually it was just talked about around the fireside, over generation to generation, passed down, until finally it comes down to Moses, who writes it down.

But nothing could be further from the truth.

A number of years ago, when I was writing **Babylon Religion**, Brother Kent Hovind contacted me, and mentioned that he saw things as labels of different books in Genesis, compiled histories, as it were. And the labels were these words: "Elleh toledoth," "These are the generations." Well, that's a label you find in Genesis 2, 5, 6, 10, 11, 25, 36 and 37.

Genesis 2:4, for instance, says,

> "These are the generations of the heavens and the earth when they were created, in the day the LORD God made the earth and the heavens…"

In Genesis 5 it starts out,

> "This is the book (sefer) of the generations of Adam."

Do you think that maybe this "book" is something Noah carried with him on the ark? I mean, after all, these five chapters of Genesis probably could fit in a 450-foot boat. You know —reading material.

But is there something in the Bible that gives us an end-date, after which something before it could not have been written? Yes, as a matter of fact.

If I tell you something "**is** there" or "**was** there," it means different things, doesn't it? If I say something "**was** there," and "**did** this," then whether it's still there and still does this is anybody's guess, right?

But if I write something down, saying it "**is** there" and "**does** this," then at the time I wrote those words, anybody else could come up and read it and say, "Yeah, it **is** there, and it **does** this."

Look at Genesis 2:10-11:

> "And a river went out (past tense) of Eden to water the garden; and from thence it was parted (past tense) and became into four heads. The name of the first *is* Pison: that *is* it which compasseth the whole land of Havilah, where *there is* gold;"

Now, "is" is not in the Hebrew. So don't count "is." That's why it's in italics in the King James.

But look at that other word in verse 11: "***compasseth***" — present tense. Compass, you know, to go around something. That's why we use a compass to draw circles.

Compasseth what? The "land of Havilah."

A lot of people think "Havilah" was located in Arabia. If you look at a map of Arabia, do you see any river compassing "Havilah, where there is gold?"

No? Well, neither do I.

Now let's look at verse 13:

> "And the name of the second river *is* Gihon: the same *is* it that **compasseth** (present tense) the whole land of Ethiopia."

Some people think the river Nile was the Gihon, and somehow it meandered around Ethiopia. Other people say, "No, Ethiopia is 'Cush,' and therefore Cush could have been in another place."

But one thing is true, no matter what you do: ***It's not there now, is it?*** So when did it go away? The Bible leaves us one, big, obvious answer: Noah's flood. That one event changed the geography of the entire world.

If the written record of creation was carried by someone on Noah's ark, then it had to have been preserved after that.

You know how we know? We have it! There's no other explanation, right?

And Moses couldn't have written it in the present tense, because it wasn't there when he was on top of Mount Sinai. That would have been a lie. So Moses didn't write it.

If it was preserved through the Flood, and preserved after the Flood, it is conceivable it was passed down by one generation to another. And more "books" were added to it, or one "book" was added afterward in succeeding generations, say from godly Shem, then through to Abraham, Isaac, and Jacob; then maybe Levi. That would explain Moses (from the tribe of Levi), and then him writing the Pentateuch, and passing it down through the tribe of Levi, according to God's word.

Under inspiration, then, Moses wrote the Torah scroll, compiling the old information, plus the information that God revealed to him on Mount Sinai. And all together, that is called the Torah. And the first book of the Torah we call "Genesis."

A God who went through all that to preserve His words —the Fall of man, the Flood of mankind, Moses and the wilderness, and the kings and all that— that is a God who could preserve His words from that day to this day. And do you know what? In English, we have it. It's called the King James Bible, God's preserved words.

First, God promised to preserve His words. Then God gave us examples of what kind of God He is. That makes us trust Him when 4000 years after creation His Son said,

> "Heaven and earth shall pass away, but my words shall not pass away." (Matt. 24:35; Mark 13:31; Luke 21:33)

He preserved those same faith-building words, starting with the words that He spoke to Adam in Genesis 1 all the way to the words He spoke to John in Revelation 22. And God preserved His words through His faithful followers.

Isn't that awesome?

14

This Bible Is History, Not Myth

How many times have you heard that the Bible is a myth? Or that it is a book of myths? It may have been at college, by a friend, a relative or even a minister. I've had my fill of those. How about you? Would you like to have an answer for that accusation?

The secular world wants you to believe that as we evolved into more "civilized" people, ancient superstitious myths of gods got formalized into moral stories that teach a point, a lesson. But, of course, nobody actually believes that they happened. Actually, it's quite the opposite.

On page 64 of ***Babylon Religion: How a Babylonian Goddess Became the Virgin Mary***, I tell one of the "Secrets of Babylon Religion." First, let's start in Romans 1:25. It talks about people:

> "Who ***changed*** the truth of God ***into*** a lie, and worshipped and served the creature more than the Creator, who is blessed for ever. Amen."

So they started with the truth. Then they made changes until it was a lie. But how can you tell what ***is*** the truth of God? Only if you have the unchanged words of God!

As I wrote in ***Babylon Religion***:

> "But the words of God are the only way to tell God's truth from the Devil's lies! No wonder we have so many religions! At first the priests didn't need to write down the "mysteries" they taught. Why should they? They were making it up as they went along in the first place! So historical fact de-evolved into legend and myth:"

First, there's the HISTORICAL EVENT. It's typically related to others in the form of a STORY. But a story, when it is not written down soon after the events happened, gets exaggerated into a LEGEND.

This makes people look better and more important than they are. If this continues, the legend is blown up like a balloon into a MYTH. Suddenly the real people turn into "gods" and are worshipped —usually for selfish reasons, like money or good crops.

Myths are the evidence of de-evolution, not things getting better.

So, let's apply this to the Bible. Does the Bible qualify as a myth? Not at all! Here's why.

Exodus 20 starts out: "And God spake ***all these words***, saying,"

At the end of the 40 years of wandering in the wilderness, God says through Moses in Deuteronomy 12:28: "Observe and hear ***all these words*** which I command thee..."

Even at the end, or into the Babylonian Captivity, 500s BC, God provided His words to them. God said through Jeremiah:

> "So Jeremiah wrote in a book all the evil that should come upon Babylon, even ***all these words*** that are written against Babylon." (Jeremiah 51:60)

God calls ***these words*** "scripture":

> "All scripture is given by inspiration of God, and is profitable for doctrine, for reproof, for correction, for instruction in righteousness: That the man of God may be perfect, throughly furnished unto all good works." (2 Timothy 3:16)

So, God's words —all of them— are scripture. And Jesus Himself said:

> "Heaven and earth shall pass away, but my words shall not pass away." (Matthew 24:35)

God's words never left the initial "story" stage. God froze it right there. Historical events were permanently written down as a STORY. End of story!

God's holy Book of His words, the Bible, is unlike any book in history. It is God's exact words without man's extra interpretation.

That's why you want God's literal words, not a paraphrase, and you want God's complete words, nothing added, and nothing taken away. The only English Bible that meets those qualifications as God's complete and holy words is the King James Bible.

The Bible is a Book unlike any other book. It's also the only Book that tells you about different civilizations and places and events, over thousands of years, where you can dig and find the evidence.

No other book does that. It is the foundation of modern science, archaeology, anthropology, geology, even law as we have it today. Its fulfilled prophecies have even turned atheists and agnostics, skeptics, lawyers and judges into believers.

It is a Book that covers 4,000 years of history, without a mistake. It's the opposite of a myth! It is the most historically reliable and verifiable Book in all history!

This King James Bible is the finest example of absolute and unchanged truth in existence.

15

You Can Know the Line between God's Words and Man's

A lot of brothers and sisters have written to me, asking, "What study Bible do you recommend?" Thanks. You just put me in a minefield. Would you like to learn how to navigate your way out, one step at a time? Let's see if this helps.

Rule #1: Know your authority. What do you rely on? You want to be sure that you have God's words. That's why you must have a King James Bible —not a King James II, III, 21, not a New King James, American, Modern, not a Comfort-able, not an Expositor's, not a New Scofield, just a plain, ordinary King James Bible. And prayer. And the Lord will bless you. You need to know what words are God's and what words are man's. Otherwise, you step on a landmine. *BOOM!*

Rule #2: What is your purpose? Every study Bible was created for a purpose. What's your purpose for a study Bible? What do you want the study Bible to do for you? Do you want it to teach you doctrine? Do you want it to teach you history or prophecy or archaeology? Do you want helpful life-applications? Do you want it to help you win others to Christ?

Then you need to know…

Rule #3: Every author is biased. He has his own point of view. He's showing you what he thinks, and what he thinks you and I should think. That's why he wrote it in a study Bible. That's true, for example, with a Prophecy study Bible that I have which is no longer available in the King James version. You have to compromise and get a New King James.

But remember Rule #1? Know your authority. Insist on a King James.

Question everything else. Want it to teach you science? Remember Rule #3: whether creation or even archaeology, every author is biased. They will try to sway you to believe or doubt the way they believe or doubt.

That's why they put their words, again, in a study Bible. Being in a Bible makes it seem more, well, biblical. And that makes the study Bible seem like it's an authority.

But never forget Rule #1. The KJV is your authority, not the notes. For example, I have an archaeological study Bible, and it's available in NIV and King James. I actually have both. The notes in both are basically just the same. So being in even a King James Bible does not mean that the notes are more conservative or even more accurate or more authentic.

Do you want help with modern life? Think of a Life Application Bible —a perfect example. Remember, they are also in multiple versions. They try to apply scriptural principles in your daily life. But again, multiple versions violate Rule #1, authority, and they are biased —Rule #3, the notes basically don't change between the versions.

So, what about the kitchen sink? Do you want the kitchen sink? There are some kitchen sink study Bibles that are not about any one thing. In fact, it seems that they tried to squeeze as much as possible between the covers without it exploding.

They try to take an entire Bible college education and

cram it between those two covers. And every one of them is what? Rule #3: Biased!

So,

Rule #1: Know your authority.

Rule #2: Know your purpose.

Rule #3: All authors are biased.

You have just avoided a lot of land mines.

Let me give you some more navigation helps. For instance, **Maps.** You want to know where an event took place. Modern map-making is getting much more accurate.

One of the reasons you want to have accurate maps is you want to be able to tell height and depth. Because when the Bible says "up" it means "up," not "north." When it says, "they went down," it means they went down. The directions in a Bible are exactly literal.

Second, **Charts.** You want to learn, and it's fun to learn, months, festivals, money, miracles, parables, and timelines, things like that. I have illustrations that I love of the temple and the tabernacle. I love to look at them. But they should have a feature to point you back to the scriptures from which they are found.

In addition, I like to have, and you want to have in a study Bible, an **Index** to the notes of the study Bible, as well as a good **Concordance.** Make it as big as possible. You want to find the verse, right? And if you don't find it big enough in here, then do what I do, and have a Bible program on your cell phone so you can just look up the verse and find what you need to find.

What if you want a study Bible that is not in the King James, or you want one that is *not* King James? You have nothing you can rely upon... at all! You must at least keep a

King James nearby, and open, to correct these study Bibles' ***many*** mistakes.

Remember, these study Bibles are tricky, and they are deceptive. With a King James Bible, you need to know where the Scripture stops. That is where God's words, truth, stops and man's words, opinions, begin.

Let's review:

Rule #1:
Know your authority. Have the King James Bible.

Rule #2:
Know your purpose. Every study
Bible has a purpose.

Rule #3:
Every author is biased.

And two more:

Rule #4:
Believe everything God says, whether
you understand it or not, and...

Rule #5:
Question everything man wrote. No exceptions.

16

Muslims Can't Use It against You

You know why Muslims love Bible versions? Because they do the work *for* them, to pull away Christians toward Islam. Want to see an example?

I once received a letter from a Bible-believing friend who had recently encountered a Muslim. But this wasn't like any ordinary encounter with a Muslim.

My friend told me that the Muslim man came up to him crying. My friend said, "I could see the tears forming in his [the Muslim's] eyes as he explained to me how if he hadn't accepted the tract ***This Was Your Life*** and some other tracts I'd given him a week later, he would still have been bowing to the false god Allah!"

He then said that he **had been** a Christian, but Muslims had won him over.... (are you ready for this?) ...on the ***Bible*** version issue!

They told him, "Look, just compare all the false god Christian bibles and what do you find? ***Confusion***, right? The Christians themselves say that God is not the author of confusion. So, by their own words they are ***liars*** serving confusion!"

My friend adds, "This man then ***forced his family*** to become Muslim and to bow to Allah."

It was because of my friend giving the Muslim the Chick

tracts and showing him that we *do* have one preserved Bible, in English, the King James Bible, that he told his family he was wrong and is now going to take them over to a Christian Church.

"He said that if it weren't for giving him all the little books, he may have lifted his eyes in Hell!" The repentant Muslim thanked my friend. He was crying, and my friend was crying!

But wait a minute. Do Muslims really use the Bible version issue to pull away Christians toward Islam? I checked a number of Muslim sites myself, on the web. Guess what? They like to use 1 Corinthians 14:33 (the first part, anyway): "For God is not the author of confusion, but of peace..."

Just like the Muslim man said, they call multiple Bible versions "confusion." And you know what? They're right! God is *not* the author of confusion.

He intended for one Bible to be in one language. And in English, thank God, we have it: the King James Bible; over 400 years tried, tested and proved.

Okay, so Muslims did use the Bible version issue to pull that one Christian away from his faith and toward Islam. But what about the man on the street? Let me tell you about my son.

My son goes witnessing on the street to anyone who will talk to him. And he witnesses to a number of Muslims of all ages. And guess what? Almost every single one says the same thing: "God's not the author of confusion. You have multiple Bible versions. That's proof that you guys don't have the truth."

So they say: "Well, you all believe in all these different Bibles that change and are different." And my son says, "No.

Many people do, but I don't." And they say, "Well, what Bible do you read? The King James Bible?" And he says, "As a matter of fact, I do!"

And that's it. End of discussion. It opens the door, and then my son can witness to them, because he said, "No, God kept His promise. God preserved His words for us in English. And this is *it*."

I have been a Bible-believer for over 34 years and used all kinds of Bibles. And I'll tell you this: all the many Bible versions that I read before brought more questions than answers.

But in the 15 years that I've been trusting God's preserved words in English, the King James Bible, I've had more answers than questions.

17

"Original Autographs Only" Changes Doctrine

The Presbyterian Church (USA) has decided that God's okay with them marrying homosexuals. The members of the PCUSA are not so okay with it.

One brother in Christ really got the point through by telling a story about his childhood. He tells the story of when he was a little boy. He was taught that God's holy word was the final authority. That fascinated him! I can imagine his mom telling him that's why in their church they would always find the King James Bible in the pews.

Anyway, he wanted to find out if this were true. So, he got on his bicycle and went through town from church to church, opened the door, and walked in the back, and checked the pews to see what they had (that was before the churches locked their doors, of course).

And guess what he found? Most of the churches did have King James Bibles. Now there were some Presbyterian churches that had gotten the RSV (Revised Standard Version) and the Episcopal church had the Book of Common Prayer.

But this exercise in his childhood taught him that, as he said it, "God's word was very special."

Anyway, years passed. Here's what this brother wrote:

"When things started to go wrong in this country, I noticed a lot of finger pointing and blame stating and sharing, however, things continued to get worse until I once again found myself examining the church as a child seeking answers. What I found were many different Bibles. Many different versions and to my recent knowledge, none of the King James Bibles that I remember dominating once, being found.

"What happened? This put me into an investigating mode that lasted two years. To my astonishment, I found that the churches had given in to the Scholar's decree that although we have copies of the originals, we don't have the originals. Therefore, the truth could be interpreted in different ways.

"What??? No wonder so many students feeling the call of God in their lives came away from Seminary discouraged, betrayed, and yes, some of them given over to agnostic interpretations and even atheistic thought. Where is that firm foundation?"

Then he quoted Jeremiah 6:16:

"Thus saith the LORD, Stand ye in the ways, and see, and ask for the old paths, where is the good way, and walk therein, and ye shall find rest for your souls. But they said, We will not walk therein."

This brother concluded:

"And there, my brethren, is where the problem lies. We have abandoned the pure word of God for man's interpretation. The deceitfulness of man has made merchandise of us all."

God gave us His words. And He preserved them for us in a Book, a Holy Book, so that we can believe it and live by it.

As this brother pointed out: "God never intended for us to rewrite it."

We cannot let our preachers and teachers and pastors get away with taking away God's words, changing God's words, and adding on man's words. This —ordaining homosexuals and performing gay marriages— is a consequence of abandoning the words that God gave in favor of man's "preferences" and interpretations. And, of course, that is just a part of the set-up for one world religion and one world Bible for that one world religion.

Brothers and sisters, we need to stand up for God's holy words, for us in English, the King James Bible. We need to read them, believe them, teach them and spread them.

18

You Can Know What You Believe

When I came to believe with all my heart that God had kept His promise to preserve His words, and that those words were perfectly preserved in the King James Bible, I cried off and on for 24 hours. Do you want to know why?

I cried because I have a Bachelor of Arts in Bible and Linguistics. I have a Masters of Divinity in General Theology with all my emphasis in Linguistics. I have years of linguistics study and Bible translation study.

I cried because I could no longer wrestle with what Metzger or the committee said in the *Textual Commentary on the Greek New Testament*, or Reinecker's *Linguistic Key to the Greek New Testament*, or Jesuit Zerwick and Grosvenor's *Grammatical Analysis of the Greek New Testament*, nor could I wrestle with the UBS 3rd or 4th edition, or the *Nestles 26th or 27th (now 28th)* edition.

But you want to have your commentaries. You want to have your books. You want to have your linguistic one-upmanship. You want to trust the men who stood on the shoulders of giants, who stood on the shoulders of other giants, who stood on the shoulders of pioneers.

You want to have that. You want to feel smart. You want to believe you are getting the newest advances of the most advanced knowledge.

And then you find out that some guy who got raised up with the King James Bible was way ahead of you. Because he already knew what he believed.

And I had no idea what I believed. I had to start all over again, after 18 years. That's why I cried over a 24-hour period. But I did start over, and with faith, not doubt. And I did grow in faith, instead of doubt. And that's why I am able to hold my King James Bible up high and say, "I may not understand every word of my King James Bible, but I believe every word of my King James Bible."

You can't buy that kind of faith.

> "So then faith cometh by hearing, and hearing by the word of God." (Romans 10:17)

So, you'd better make sure that what you have *is* the word of God, and then put your faith in it! Even if you have to start all over again, from ground zero, you'll never regret it.

19

You Can Learn from the True Church Fathers

I am sad to report that in 2014 Ulf Ekman, a major charismatic leader in Sweden, with a congregation of over 3,000 and a ministry that has reached over 100,000, became a Roman Catholic.

So did Alex Jones (not the internet personality —an American pastor), along with 62 members of his former congregation. They literally closed the church and joined the Catholic church. And Jones even wrote a book about it.

You know the old saying, "All roads lead to Rome?" What road did these guys take that led them to Rome? According to their own testimony, a lot of what gave them their direction was reading and believing the writings of the Roman Catholic "Church Fathers."

Who are these "Church Fathers," and how did they lead these guys to Rome? The people called "Church Fathers" were early Catholic leaders who wrote about the Bible and early doctrines that were being formulated, taught, and debated for the Catholic "Church."

When I was at Fuller Seminary, they divided the "Church Fathers" into groups to make it easy. The major dividing line was the first Roman Catholic Council: Constantine's Council of Nicaea in 325 AD. All the writers that came before

325 are called Ante-Nicene and the ones at and after 325 are Nicene and Post-Nicene Fathers.

They also distance them, or divide them, by how far they are from the apostles themselves. So, they are called "Apostolic Fathers" if they wrote in Greek, within the first 3 generations after the apostles died.

And then there are "Latin Fathers" and there are "Greek Fathers," based on the language in which they wrote.

But don't be deceived. Despite what the Catholic system says, there is no such thing as the "Unanimous consent of the Church Fathers." That's just a lot of hooey. These aren't fathers of the church! They didn't "father" the church!

That was done a long time before, by the Lord Jesus Christ, long before these guys were even born. They only "fathered" Roman Catholicism, luring people away from the scriptures and into the opinions of men.

But I do read and believe the true Church Fathers. You want to know which ones? Matthew, Mark, Luke, John, Peter, Paul, James and Jude. These are the real church fathers.

These are the men who wrote by the inspiration of God. What they wrote is absolutely infallible. And they totally agree with one another, as all 40+ authors do, in the Bible. They're the only true "Church Fathers."

But I don't really like to call them fathers. Instead, I like to do what Jesus said:

> "And call no man your father upon the earth: for one is your Father, which is in heaven." (Matthew 23:9)

20

It Gets Death and Hell Right

Is the King James Bible all wrong about death and hell?

After all that I have said about the new Bibles removing the word "hell" and some of the words about hell, I was amazed to find out about a new accusation (at least, to me): Some people are teaching the King James is dangerous, because of the times that it doesn't translate the Hebrew שְׁאוֹל (Sheol) or the Greek ᾅδης (Hades) as hell! And that the cultists just love to use the King James because of this supposed "mistake."

Is it true? Is the King James Bible a goldmine for groups that don't believe in hell? What's the real story? I had to know.

First, I actually heard a scholarly guy claim: "Hades is not the grave. No Greek or Hebrew scholar would say that it is."

Okay, the accusation that the King James translates Hades as "grave" all over the place is just wrong. Hades only appears in the New Testament 11 times. And 10 times of the 11 it is translated "hell." Just one time it is translated "grave":

> "O death, where is thy sting? O grave, where is thy victory?" (1 Corinthians 15:55)

This is not talking about rescuing people from punishment in hell, is it? Of course not! Hebrews 9:27 says:

> "And as it is appointed unto men once to die, but after this the judgment:"

Everyone will be judged after they die. They don't get rescued out of the torments of hell. For the unforgiven, it's hell, then judgment, then the lake of fire. "Out of the frying pan and into the lake of fire."

So, it's talking about the afterlife, but it's not talking about torments of hell. So how do we translate that? It's the same Greek word Hades. But it's not about hell as we English-speakers understand it —which is always negative.

They could have used a lot of words, but they chose to use the word "grave," to encompass when they're put in the ground, and they descend into the afterlife, whether paradise, called "Abraham's bosom," or torments, what we call "hell."

Believe it or not, this wasn't new with the King James translators. The Bishops Bible translates Sheol and Hades the same way, with the same words. That was something the King James translators didn't have to fix. The Bishops Bible translators already got that right!

1 Corinthians 15:55 is a direct reference to Hosea 13:14:

> "I will ransom them from the power of the grave; I will redeem them from death: O death, I will be thy plagues; O grave, I will be thy destruction…"

Grave, of course, is Sheol. So now we come to the Hebrew side.

God never promised to ransom people from torments in hell. But did He promise to rescue us from death itself, from the afterlife, and from our estrangement from God? Absolutely! That was their hope! Without the cross and forgiveness of sins and being granted Christ's righteousness, they could not go to heaven.

So literally, without the gospel, they could not be made perfect. That's why it says in Hebrews 11:39-40:

It Gets Death and Hell Right

> "And these all, having obtained a good report through faith, received not the promise: God having provided some better thing for us, that they without us should not be made perfect."

So they stayed in "the grave" –the afterlife, but not in torment of hell– until Jesus set the captives free and "led captivity captive," (See Psalm 68:18 and Ephesians 4:8.)

"Okay," you may say. "You proved how some people translated Hades as "the grave" in that one New Testament verse. But what about the 31 verses in the Old Testament that Sheol was translated 'the grave'?"

Great question. Totally fair.

Let's look at the very first time the King James translators ever translated Sheol as "the grave." Genesis 37:35. "And all his sons and all his daughters rose up to comfort him; but he refused to be comforted; and he said, For I will go down into the grave unto my son mourning. Thus his father wept for him."

The word for "grave" here is Sheol. But are there any other English translations that are willing to translate Sheol as "the grave" in this verse? Yes!

Sheol was translated "the grave" in over 15 translations, including:

The NIV (1984 and 2011),

The New Living Translation (1996, 2004, 2007),

The New King James (1982);

And 5 Jewish Bibles, including:

The Complete Jewish Bible (1998),

Jewish Publication Society (JPS) 1917,

Rabbi Isaac Leeser Bible (1853),

Over 15 translations, 5 of them Jewish, that had no

problems, based on context, of defining Sheol as the "grave." And I doubt that anyone would argue that they weren't scholars.

Translating Sheol and Hades by two words, "hell" and "the grave," depending on the context, is nothing new. We have lots of words in English that have more than one meaning, depending upon how they're used.

There are 31 verses where Sheol is translated "grave." But there are also 31 verses where Sheol is translated "hell."

Other Bible versions minimize hell, by leaving Sheol and Hades untranslated, with "hell" in the Bible only a few times, or leaving it out altogether!

Which would you rather have: A Bible that removes "hell" altogether, and refuses to translate the Hebrew Sheol and the Greek Hades? Or one that clearly communicates the intent of each passage?

21

It Destroys What the Devil Wants

The Devil destroys lives by getting people on a four-step path. Would you like to know how it starts?

What does the Devil want? He wants to get you off the path of faith and onto the path of doubt. He doesn't care how far on the doubt path you are, as long as you're off the path of faith.

To know what the four steps are on Satan's path of doubt, we need look no further than Genesis.

God gave Adam and Eve a paradise. It was everything they could possibly want with only one restriction. God said to Adam:

> "But of the tree of the knowledge of good and evil, thou shalt not eat of it: for in the day that thou eatest thereof thou shalt surely die." (Genesis 2:17)

The Devil decided to pick on the one person who wasn't there when God said that: Eve. In Genesis 3:1, one day Eve is in the garden and the snake says:

> "... Yea, hath God said, Ye shall not eat of every tree of the garden?" (Genesis 3:1)

Eve thinks, "Wait. Was it 'every tree,' or 'any tree'? What was it Adam said that God said? Augh!" She was confused.

Step 1: Confusion about the words of God.

> "And the woman said unto the serpent, We may eat of the fruit of the trees of the garden: But of the fruit of the tree which is in the midst of the garden, God hath said, Ye shall not eat of it, neither shall ye touch it, lest ye die." (Genesis 3:2-3)

Time out! 2 errors:

1. There were two trees in the middle of the garden, not just one.
2. God didn't say Adam and Eve couldn't touch it.

He just said "thou shalt not eat of it." Eve was confused.
Step 1: Confusion, complete.
Step 2: Doubt.
The Devil didn't miss a beat:

> "And the serpent said unto the woman, Ye shall not surely die: For God doth know that in the day ye eat thereof, then your eyes shall be opened, and ye shall be as gods, knowing good and evil." (Genesis 3:4-5)

"God has a secret you don't know! La, la, la la, la!" Satan was taunting Eve. "Bottom line, Eve, God doesn't have your best interests at heart."

"God doesn't want you to know what He knows."

And then he implies, so gently, "Yesssssss, but I do..." And that was it. He was gone. He'd done his job. He could hit the road, because Eve could do the rest of it herself.

Eve had started to doubt her own Creator.

How do I know?

1. She didn't ask her husband what the Lord said.
2. She didn't wait until the Lord started walking through the garden, to ask Him herself what He had said.

Eve doubted what she really needed to know: God's exact words. And she doubted that God had her best interests at heart.

Step 2: Doubt, complete.

Step 3: Disbelief.

> "And out of the ground made the LORD God to grow every tree that is pleasant to the sight, and good for food; the tree of life also in the midst of the garden, and the tree of knowledge of good and evil." (Genesis 2:9)

So every other tree of the garden was pleasant to the sight, and good for food.

But those two trees were all that was left, in the middle of the garden. She could have whatever tree she desired. Only one was forbidden.

But look at this:

> "And when the woman saw that the tree was good for food, and that it was pleasant to the eyes, **and a tree to be desired to make one wise**, …" (Genesis 3:6)

Wait a second.

God never said it was desirable to make you wise.

God said if you eat of it, you're going to die!

So she decided she wasn't going to believe what God said and His exact words, or even check them for herself. She was going to believe the Devil, that *he* had her best interests at heart?

So now, Eve thought it was desirable to make her wise.

Eve, don't you believe God?

No, she didn't.

Step 3: Disbelief, complete.

Step 4: Rebellion.

Let's go back to Genesis 3:6:

> "...she took of the fruit thereof, and did eat, and gave also unto her husband with her; and he did eat."

She decided, "I'm gonna do it my own way. God doesn't have my best interests at heart. I don't trust those words. I'll look after my own best interests."

She rebelled. She took of the forbidden fruit. And BANG! **Step 4: Rebellion,** complete.

There you have it, the Four Steps of the Devil to ruin your life and get you off the path of faith and onto the path of doubt.

And it starts with confusion about God's exact words.

But getting onto that path is getting onto a path of sin.

Romans 14:23 says:

> "...for whatsoever is not of faith is sin."

God wants us to have faith.

> "But without faith it is impossible to please him: for he that cometh to God must believe that he is, and that he is a rewarder of them that diligently seek him." (Hebrews 11:6)

So the Devil wants you off the path of faith, on the path of doubt.

It comes in 4 phases:

1. **Confusion** over God's words, then
2. **Doubt**
3. **Disbelief**
4. **Rebellion**

It Destroys What the Devil Wants

He doesn't care what step you're on, as long as you're *off* the path of faith.

Get on the path of faith!

Stay on the path of faith: God's preserved words in English, the King James Bible. Believe them. Trust God's words. He has your best interests at heart, and you can believe His every word.

Accept nothing less.

22

The Text Critics Have to Change History to Reject It

I was so excited when I found a book at House of Bibles in Fullerton, a few miles from my old Bible College! It was *The Text of the Earliest New Testament Greek Manuscripts: New and Complete Transcriptions with Photographs*, edited by Philip Comfort and David Barrett.

This was the first copy of parts of 65-70 papyrus manuscripts I had ever been able to get hold of.

My copy, made by Tyndale House Publishers, has not stood the test of time. 15 years later, it was totally coming apart. But there's some stuff I really want you to see.

I'm just going to focus on pages 27 and 28. In these pages you are about to see some secrets of Textual Criticism.

1) Text Critics change the terms so you wouldn't trust God's words if you found them.

2) Text Critics lie about what the Alexandrian and Preserved Texts really are.

3) Text Critics aren't looking for the same Bible that you and I are looking for.

Take a look at what they said in their own words.

Text Critics who are against the King James usually pit

The Text Critics Have to Change History to Reject It

the KJV against the Alexandrian Text.

How many parts or complete Greek manuscripts are we talking about? I have a book on the Sinaiticus by the British Library in London, called *In a Monastery Library* (2006). On page 35, it says:

> "According to the authoritative list maintained by the Institute for New Testament Studies at Münster, there are 5746 surviving manuscripts of parts of the New Testament in Greek, including 118 papyri."

45 papyri have been claimed as Alexandrian. But when I checked Rylands Greek papyrus p52, for myself, I found nothing in the text to indicate which it is, preserved or Alexandrian. That brings the number for me down to 44 Alexandrian manuscripts.

44 out of a total of 5746 is .00765 or 7/10 of 1% that favor the Alexandrian Text. Even if you round up, it's just 8/10 of 1% on their side. It doesn't make much of a difference.

So at least 99.235% of the evidence is stacked against the Alexandrian Text. That's a lot of evidence, don't you think?

But publishers use that 8/10 of 1% to go against the whole history of preservation and create most of the modern Bibles you see today. All this from that tiny smattering of Gnostic desert discards and modern counterfeits they call the Alexandrian Text.

Isn't that incredible?

How can they do that?

Let me show you.

Here's Secret #1. When they talk about manuscripts that are like our King James, they call them "Byzantine Manuscripts." Why do they use that term? Because they teach that Emperor Constantine set a standard text for the Bible at a huge meeting in about 330 AD. Never mind that there is absolutely no evidence for this meeting having anything to do with determining what was and wasn't scripture.[7] "Westcott and Hort said so. Therefore, it must be true!"

So then, for them, the "Byzantine Period" started about 330 AD. But what if you find older copies of scripture that are like those later copies? Isn't that evidence that those "Byzantine Bibles" are actually in the line of God's preserved words?

Not to the Text Critics. Because of that made-up term, they throw those manuscripts out the window! Here are the actual words of Comfort and Barrett, the authors, page 27:

> "For starters, the 'Byzantine' category can be eliminated. None of the early papyri are Byzantine, because they antedate [were made before] the Byzantine period."

That means that if you have an older copy of the scriptures that looks the same as the ones we call Byzantine, we'll say it's not really the same. It just looks the same as those Byzantine Bibles.

It's like saying, "There are no dinosaurs in the Bible, because the term 'dinosaur' is not in the Bible." Of course not! The term "dinosaur" wasn't invented until 1842! But there WAS a term for those giant lizard animals before 1842: "dragon." And "dragon" is in the Bible 34 times!

"Byzantine Text" is an invented term, just like the term "dinosaur."

Comfort and Barrett continue:

---

7) See note in chapter 9.

> "If some of them happen to display some Byzantine qualities (such as expansion and harmonization), these manuscripts simply display scribal tendencies manifest in full during the Byzantine era."

Let's take apart their sneaky words. Text Critics mention two "Byzantine qualities." First is "expansion." Critics mean it "adds words." But that's backwards. Actually, the Alexandrian text takes away words. So it's not that so-called "Byzantine texts" have stuff added to them. It's that the Alexandrian texts have stuff cut out of them.

The second term was "harmonization." Text Critics mean copyists changed scriptures in different verses so that they mean the same thing. But that's backwards. What it really means is the words of God don't contradict each other.

So, what are the Text Critics looking for? Turn those words around. They are looking for a shortened, contradictory text. That's what those code words really mean.

But, let's not use the Text Critics' made-up term "Byzantine." God promised to preserve His words, so let's use the term Preserved Line of texts. That makes everything much more clear.

The definition of Preserved is: manuscripts that are the same as what the original writers wrote under inspiration by the Holy Ghost. Now, any manuscript could be one of the Preserved Line, if it says the same thing that God originally inspired.

But Text Critics redefine the Preserved Line and call it "Byzantine," so they can dismiss it.

You can't win with these guys. If these Bible-doubters found the actual words of Paul, in his own handwriting, they would throw it out of consideration as an original autograph.

They'd say, "It displays Byzantine scribal tendencies."

So what? It's the actual words of Paul! It's the words of God, not some "Byzantine text." So "Byzantine text" is one of those "weasel words." They weasel their way out of trusting God's actual words preserved through history, by renaming the Preserved Text "Byzantine."

Text Critics are NOT looking for the Preserved Text. They'd be out of a job! We already have it. In English, it's the King James Bible. Not much left to criticize, here.

So what kind of text ARE Text Critics looking for? They are looking for the Alexandrian Text.

Look at what Comfort and Barrett wrote on page 28:

> "The Alexandrian text is found in manuscripts produced by scribes trained in Alexandrian scribal practices, the best of its kind in Greco-Roman times. Such scribes were schooled in producing well-crafted, accurate copies."

How well-crafted and accurate does the Alexandrian Text on the next page look?

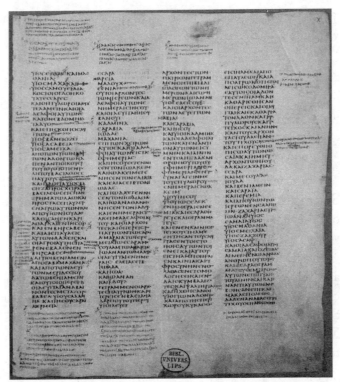

Remember, they say this is one of the "oldest and best," Codex Sinaiticus.[8]

Then they go on:

"The Proto-Alexandrian manuscripts are usually purer than the later ones in that the earlier are less polished and closer to the ruggedness of the original writings."

To a Text Critic, "less polished" and "rugged" mean the text isn't smooth. It may have mistakes. It may have bad grammar. It may not make sense.

---

8) See *Is The World's Oldest Bible A Fake?* for more information.

My Greek teacher told us that the Apostle John made writing mistakes. Textual Criticism proved it to him!

Wow.

Back to Barrett and Comfort.

> "In short, these manuscripts display the work of scribes who had the least creative interaction with the text —they stayed with their task of making good copies."

If you want to see examples of the "good copy" called Sinaiticus, see *Is the 'World's Oldest Bible' a Fake?* Or check out the video series, "Something Funny about Sinaiticus" on youtube.com/c/chicktracts.

The "Alexandrian" manuscripts remove words, phrases and verses that change doctrine, on top of all the rest. So, in certain verses, Jesus Christ isn't God, or Jesus became God's Son after He was baptized to forgive His sins, like it says in Mark chapter 1 in Sinaiticus. That's pretty "creative interaction," don't you think?

Of course, it won't earn them any brownie points on Judgment Day.

Modern Text Critics are looking for a "rough text," that is, incomplete, inconsistent, and contradictory. They are looking for a man-made text.

Bible believers believe God's own promise to preserve His own words. They are looking for a preserved, clean, pure text. They don't want one changed by doubting men.

The text they are looking for is not rough, but "smooth." That is, it's complete, consistent, and it doesn't contradict itself. It has a consistent Gospel and Jesus Christ properly exalted as God the Son.

And it shows a clear Godhead and the way to salvation.

And it tells the truth about heaven, hell, angels, devils, and faith in Christ's shed blood to get us to heaven, not good works to earn heaven.

Bible believers want a text that has been Preserved and blessed by God's "singular care and providence." That means God provided a cared-for and preserved text.

You see the difference? Bible-believers and Bible-doubters can never get together, because they are looking for different texts!

Bible-believers are looking for one that makes sense. Bible-doubters, Text Critics, are looking for one that doesn't make sense.

Look, if these Bible-doubters found John's Gospel and Epistles, in the Apostle John's own handwriting, they would set them aside, saying "It is too polished. It doesn't exhibit the rough characteristics we are looking for. It is consistent. And it makes too much sense."

That, brothers and sisters, is the secret of Textual Criticism. The Text Critics are Bible-doubters. Their definition of what the Bible is, is all wrong.

We aren't looking for a rough, inconsistent, doubt-inducing, man-made Bible.

We are looking for a smooth, consistent, faith-building, God-preserved Bible. I want what God has preserved through the ages, "by His singular care and providence," as the Westminster Confession has said since 1646. I want those faithfully preserved words in English, as the 1657 Confession says.

Remember: the doctrine of God's preserved words in English is *not* a new doctrine. It's only about 30 years younger than the King James itself.

I don't want OAO, a non-existent "original autographs only" Bible. Remember, *that* is a new doctrine. It was invented in April of 1881. It's only 4 months older than the doubters' Bible it was made for, the English Revised Version New Testament of Westcott and Hort.

Make your own choice.

Bible-believer, or Bible-doubter?

Believe God, or trust the Text Critics?

23

Publishers Plant Doubt to Make More Money

Why would a publisher, selling King James Bibles to King James Bible readers, write notes in it to make you doubt the King James Bible? Is there something in it for them? Or are they just afraid of the King James Bible? Or both?

Let's find out!

I'm going to give a few examples of the bible-doubting footnotes in just one of the KJV study Bibles. Amazingly, these are the same Bible-doubting footnotes you'll find in the NIV, ESV, NAS, NLT and any number of other versions and their study Bibles.

When Bible-believers requested more King James Bibles, publishers met the demand by making newer KJVs and more kinds of KJVs.

But *why* did they add those same, tired, Bible-doubting footnotes to the King James Bibles? Are they trying to get people to turn away from the King James? If so, why?

I bought a copy of *The King James Study Bible*, Second Edition, copyright 1988 and 2013 by Jerry Falwell's Liberty University. It was printed by Thomas Nelson, who'd rather have you buy a New King James or another one of their Bibles.

Let's take a look at some of the notes, shall we?

Mark 16:9-20. Here is just an excerpt. It says, "Ancient manuscripts contain two different endings for Mark." And then it says, "In light of the uncertainty attached to verses 9-20, it may be advised to take care in basing doctrine upon them (especially vv. 16-18)."

My Ryrie Bible says the same thing. In fact, most modern study Bibles pretty much have that same note in them.

Why? Are they afraid some false doctrine is in the verse? No, they'll never tell you that. They'll never put *that* warning in. But they want you to be …how did they put it? Uncertain. Isn't that the opposite of faith? How weird.

Philippians 2:7 has a big note in the section about Jesus, where He became a man. But in the middle of these voluminous footnotes is the statement: "He emptied Himself."

"Emptied Himself?" The scripture in the King James is perfectly clear: "But made himself of no reputation, and took upon him the form of a servant, and was made in the likeness of men." "Emptied Himself" makes Him look like He stopped being God. Isn't that what some of those TV preachers have been saying? Hmm.

1 Thessalonians 5:22 is also clear in the King James Bible: "Abstain from all appearance of evil." But they put the inaccurate "every form of" in the margin.

"Every form of evil?" Every other place εἶδος (*eidos*, the Greek word for "appearance") appears it means "how you appear to others." Same here. So this verse is really about maintaining a good testimony, isn't it?

God isn't just saying to avoid every form of evil, or evil wherever it appears. It's saying to avoid you or me *looking like* we are doing evil! If the King James reading is so clear, why did they write the false reading in the margin?

One more: 1 John 5:7-8. Just a part of the notes here:

"...verse 8 should read simply: 'The Spirit, the water, and the blood; and the three are in agreement.' The longer versions of these verses made their way into the traditional printed Greek Testament (TR) and thus into the King James Version due to influence of the Latin Bible and only four late Greek manuscripts."

So, if they don't believe it, why did they leave it in? Because it wouldn't be a King James Bible without it. —And you wouldn't buy it!

So, next question, why didn't they hire a person who believes the King James to write the King James notes in the King James study Bible? Doesn't that make sense?

It's not like there's any shortage of believers. I told you in another chapter that most people who actually read a Bible, read a King James, regardless of what version they buy, or why.

Surely, they could find a few believers in the nation, and have them write believing notes, to show why God's perfect words are translated into English in the King James Bible. It would inspire faith, not doubt.

But if they inspire faith in the very words of the King James, what do they need other Bibles for? Publishers have a *huge* inventory of multiple versions —especially this company: Thomas Nelson and Zondervan and World were all bought by HarperCollins, under Rupert Murdoch's News Corporation, and is now called "HarperCollins Christian" —although the owners are not Christian, not by a long shot.

That's over 55% of all the Bibles published, many versions. And they are scared to death of anyone or anything, including a King James with Bible-believing footnotes, interfering with their "bottom line," profits. You know, "gain," "filthy lucre," "money."

1 Timothy 6:10: "…the love of money is the root of all evil," And yes, they've got a note messing with that, too!

They love money. They love publishing KJVs, but KJVs with Bible-doubting footnotes, to get you to look at their catalog for their other Bibles and their newer versions, as well.

They're KJVs, but "Trojan Horse KJVs," with notes waiting to jump out at you and get you to doubt and question your faith, no longer believing God's holy and preserved words.

But as my old mentor said, "The scripture stops here. The rest are man's opinions."

Do believe the King James ***text***. But just don't believe the notes and the introductions. Don't let a publisher's "Trojan Horse" King James spring its trap on you.

24

It Doesn't Let You "Have it Your Way"

Breaking news: 22 fourths of Americans don't understand fractions! And another 50% don't understand statistics!

Christians tell us that 97% of Bibles all say the same thing, but that the King James Bible is the worst.

How can this be? What's hiding behind the numbers? People love to criticize, using made-up numbers to make them sound scientific. Why?

Many people read the King James Bible because it is their ONE authority. But those who criticize them can't tell you what their authority is.

Or else they look all smug and they say, "Jesus Christ is my authority!"

"Really? And where did you learn about Jesus Christ?"

"uh...the Bible."

And we're back to Square One. They're stuck, because they can't tell you which Bible gives you that ultimate authority about who Jesus Christ is.

Or else, they're like my professors, who would say, "All of the Bibles tell the truth."

But when you back them into a corner, they'll tell you: "But the King James Bible is still the worst."

Do you know why critics hate it so much? Because it isn't

a Burger King Bible. You can't just "Have it your way."

Watch!

If you read the King James Bible, and you tell them, "I read and use the King James Bible; I just don't believe it's my final authority," they'd give you an A-minus!

They don't mind if you read it or even believe it, as long as it isn't your only and ultimate authority! Don't cut in on their Burger King Bible-of-the-year or month or week!

But how could ONE BIBLE possibly be so bad? 400 years of Christians based their faith on it. And many of them have a really good track record. And they believed the words of the King James Bible (gasp!) without knowing Hebrew, Greek, Latin, German or even Aramaic!

So to you guys who say the King James Bible is so bad: I already know most of you haven't actually even read the King James. Someone, a teacher or professor just told you this line, and you believed it.

So, are you willing to read it —out loud?

Come on. Take the challenge!

The 30-day challenge. Read it out loud, for 30 days.

"But it's too hard!"

I'll let you in on a secret. Babies aren't born knowing how to read! They have to listen and learn. I know of 5-year-olds, including my kids and friends, who were reading the King James Bible at that age.

I think you're smarter than a 5-year-old.

But if you are still worried, download an audio book. Even for your phone. You can have Alexander Scourby in your ears for less than $20.

Try it. Read it OUT LOUD or have it read to you out loud, for 30 days. Then tell me how hard it is to read.

One of my friends actually took a 1611 edition with Roman type and read it aloud for 30 days. And then she came back, and she said to me, "I can understand the King James!" And her faith was lifted because she read a faith-filled version, a faith-filled Bible, not a Doubting Thomas Version.

Romans 10:17 says, "So then faith cometh by hearing, and hearing by the word of God."

What have you got to lose? Come on! I dare you! Take the 30-day challenge. And hey, if after 30 days of hearing or reading God's holy and preserved words in English, the King James Bible, you decide to go back to your Burger King Bible, you know what they say:

Have it your way.

25

Doubt: The Fruit of Textual Criticism

If Textual Criticism really brought us God's words, we would expect an explosion of faith in God. What is its fruit?

Have you ever looked inside your Bible and seen those notes that say:

"The better manuscripts do not contain this,"

"The best manuscripts do not have these verses,"

"The better manuscripts say this and not that"?

That, brothers and sisters, is called Textual Criticism. I'd like to talk to you about the fruit of Textual Criticism.

Jesus talked a lot about fruit in Matthew 7:15-20. He said:

"Beware of false prophets, which come to you in sheep's clothing, but inwardly they are ravening wolves. Ye shall know them by their fruits. Do men gather grapes of thorns, or figs of thistles? Even so every good tree bringeth forth good fruit; but a corrupt tree bringeth forth evil fruit. A good tree cannot bring forth evil fruit, neither can a corrupt tree bring forth good fruit. Every tree that bringeth not forth good fruit is hewn down, and cast into the fire. Wherefore by their fruits ye shall know them."

Doubt: The Fruit of Textual Criticism

You can't miss it from Jesus' words, can you? Fruit is what God wants, and it's ***good*** fruit.

What does God call "good fruit"? If you look in Romans 1:13, you would see that conversion of sinners is a good fruit. In 7:4, it's good works. In 15:28, it's giving to missions and to the aid of brothers and sisters in Christ who need something. Those are all good fruits that God likes.

Galatians 5:22-23, of course, is another list of good fruit: "But the fruit of the Spirit is love, joy, peace, longsuffering, gentleness, goodness, faith, meekness, temperance: against such there is no law."

That's the fruit God's looking for. Not one place in the entire Bible is ***doubt*** called a fruit. Check it for yourself. And yet this is exactly what I find in textual critics, textual criticism, and in the people strongly influenced by textual critics and textual criticism.

It's strange. If all this stuff about "getting back to the word of God" were really true, there would be **fruit** of *faith*, evangelism, giving to missions —there'd be **something!** The fruit of the Spirit!

But all I find are doubters! Like Bart Ehrman. Like Kirsopp Lake. For many years Lake followed the theories of Westcott and Hort, and Von Soden. He wrote, after years of paying attention and following their rules, "In spite of the claims of Westcott and Hort and of Von Soden, we do not know the original form of the Gospels, and it is quite likely that we ***never shall***."[9]

Then another major text scholar, Frederick Cornwallis

---

9) *Family 13 (the Ferrar Group): The Text According to Mark with a Collation of Codex 28 of the Gospels* by Kirsopp Lake, Silva Tipple Lake and Silva Lake (Christophers, 1965), p. vii. He originally wrote those words in 1941. Emphasis mine.

Conybeare, wrote this before he died in 1924: "...the ultimate text (meaning New Testament), if there ever was one that deserves to be so called, is ***forever irrecoverable***."[10]

Textual Criticism is not an act of faith. It is an act of doubt and leads only to despair.

When you see people who really believe Textual Criticism, do you see them as armed soul winners? or as armchair quarterbacks?

Do you see them fighting the enemy, or fighting the believers?

It is said that those who can, —do. Those who can't — teach. And those who can't do or teach, —are critics.

Brothers and sisters, there are only two options: faith or doubt.

I know so many people who've read the King James Bible and believe it, and the fruit is ***faith*** and acts of faith, and winning others to the faith.

Faith or doubt: it's your choice.

---

10) *History of New Testament Criticism* by F.C. Conybeare (NY: G.P. Putnam's Son, the Knickerbocker Press, 1910), p. 168). Emphasis mine.

26

It Doesn't Need "Fixing"

What if a Bible publisher asked you to "fix" the King James Bible? What would you change? How would you make it perfect? And if not "perfect," how would you make it better than it is?

Some have asked me that same question: "Would you give us a 'fixed' King James Bible?" Let me tell you something. The temptation to change God's holy and preserved words would be much too great. Change a little here, a little there...

But the only way to do that, is to make people doubt the preserved reading. It is tempting. Just ask Brother Ryrie, Brother Comfort, Brother Swaggart, Brother Green, or any of the study-Bible producers: Zondervan, Holman, Oxford, Thomas Nelson.

If it is true, why try to change it? That would be "changing the truth of God into a ... lie" (Romans 1:25). And if it isn't true, why even read it?

What "standard of truth" would we use, to change the Bible? We all report to the same Person, the One who will sit on a great white throne. It is a good idea not to get Him angry.

Don't try to change the King James. Instead, God will change your life for the better if you trust it as God's holy and preserved words in English.

27

Even the Devil Had to Use God's Exact Words

The Devil is a lot of things. But he's no dummy. Ezekiel 28:17 says, "...thou hast corrupted thy"—what? "wisdom by reason of thy brightness:" So the Devil is wise, and he knows stuff. Would you like to know something that the Devil even knows, about the scripture, the literal words of God?

When he confronted Jesus, in the Second Temptation, (Matthew 4), Satan used scripture, the absolute, infallible, undeniable words of the living God. Realize, the Devil's like a lawyer, he's prodding, he's poking, he's trying to find a chink in the Lord's armor. You can't just "make stuff up" with the Son of the living God. He knows *everything*.

Let's start in verse 5:

"Then the devil taketh him up into the holy city, and setteth him on a pinnacle of the temple,"

By the way, John 2:16, that's Jesus' Father's house (the temple). Satan sets Him on His father's house. Remember that.

Verse 6:

"And saith unto him, If thou be the Son of God, cast thyself down: for it is written, He shall give his angels charge concerning thee: and in their hands

Even the Devil Had to Use God's Exact Words 123

they shall bear thee up, lest at any time thou dash thy foot against a stone."

Satan used a scripture, this infallible scripture, the *literal* words, remember, against God.

But, see... There's a funny thing about that: When confronting the Son of God, the Devil quoted a Psalm! Psalm 91. And he used that to prove whether Jesus was "the Son of God..." What's so special about Psalm 91? Wait till you see.

Psalm 91:1 says:

"He that dwelleth in the secret place of the most High shall abide under the shadow of the Almighty."

What's "the secret place of the most High"?

And then it hit me: "The bosom of the Father." John 1:18 says:

"No man hath seen God at any time; the only begotten Son, *which is in the bosom of the Father*, he hath declared him."

Now, this just blew me away! And I was wondering, "Am I the only person who sees this?" Because if I was, I'd just set it aside.

But guess what? I found out while reading John Gill, a Baptist preacher who preceded Spurgeon, that even he saw that Psalm 91 is prophesying about the Son of God. There are lots of Psalms about Jesus as Messiah. But there aren't a lot of Psalms about Him as the Son of God.

So, this is a "protection Psalm" about God's Son while He was on the earth. That's why it says, "the only begotten Son, which is in the bosom of the Father, he hath declared him." And in Psalm 91:1 "He that dwelleth in the secret place of the most High" (the bosom of the Father), "shall abide under the shadow of the Almighty." While He is performing His earthly ministry He's going to be protected. That's amazing.

Let's get back to the Devil. He's wise. He knows his scripture. In fact, he was so wise, and thought he was so wise, he thought he was second to, or as good as, God Himself. As it says in Isaiah 14:14:

> "I will ascend above the heights of the clouds; I will be like the most High."

So, there you go. The Devil is wise. He quotes Psalm 91. And Jesus didn't call him out for bad exegesis, by the way. He went right to it. It says, instead of saying: "Yes, you're right, I lose, you win;" instead of trying to contradict him on the scripture; instead, He does something else.

You see, Psalm 91 is not the "be all, end all" of scripture. There are a lot of other scriptures. And some are very important. So, Jesus responds in Matthew, verse 7: "Jesus said unto him, It is written again, Thou shalt not tempt the Lord thy God."

It doesn't matter that the ***Lord*** promised protection for Him in His earthly life, "If thou be the Son of God." Yes, He's the Son of God. "Well, they'll bear You up." "Yes, they'll bear Me up, —BUT— "Thou shalt not tempt the Lord thy God."

You don't interfere with the plans and the purposes of God for His Son. That was the most important scripture there.

God's exact words were ***so important*** that the Devil knew he had to quote them, even to try to challenge Jesus. So how much more should we, who want to serve God, rely only upon God's exact words?

28

Your Reliable Source for Controversial Questions

I watched a clip from a popular TV program where a man was playing the president of the United States. He totally "schooled" some lady who said homosexuality was against God. He started quoting scriptures, saying that if homosexuality was against God, then so was eating shellfish, wearing two different fabrics in a garment, and sowing a field with two kinds of seed. Then he listed horrible death penalties for these sins.

He went on and on. But in the end, he sounded pretty righteous. And the woman sounded pretty stupid, using some Old Testament scriptures to condemn homosexuality.

It was dramatic. It made you gasp. But it wasn't real. It was actors acting. Writers got together certain laws that God gave Moses and then gave them a huge spin, making up horrible death penalties and said, "That'll fix those Jewish and Christian Bible believers!" And they put it on the air with false authority, since the actor was, after all, portraying a president.

Some of those laws were confined to the Jewish people. Others are for everyone, including us today. But which ones are which? And how can we know?

Are there ways to find out the difference between the

laws that God made for the purity of His chosen people Israel, and the laws that are always true, no matter who we are, throughout history? Yes, there are. And I am going to pick only one of them, using the King James Bible word, "Abomination."

Are you ready to walk through the Bible with careful eyes? Let's take apart what that president —that "TV show president" said. He referred to the scripture that calls eating shellfish an abomination.

Well, scripture calls homosexuality an abomination, too. Is eating shellfish really equal to homosexuality in Old Testament law? I looked up every verse on abomination in the whole King James Bible. This is what I found.

There are sins —39 sins I found— that God said are an abomination "to Him" or "unto Him" or "committed before Him." That means He hates it. That's one category.

But there are 2 categories of abominations. One kind is an abomination that is "to Him," "unto Him," or "committed before Him." And there is another kind that the scripture says is "unto you"—meaning the Israelites that God is keeping clean and pure for Himself.

Those are only found in one place: Leviticus 11:10-23. In Leviticus 11:12 for example, it says:

> "Whatsoever hath no fins nor scales in the waters, that shall be an abomination unto you."

—the Israelites. Leviticus 11:10-12 is about sea foods the Israelites were forbidden to eat, like eels or shellfish.

Now look at 11:23:

> "But all other flying creeping things, which have four feet, shall be an abomination unto you."

Verses 13-23 are about birds and flying insects the Israelites were forbidden to eat, birds that eat dead animals, and flies and such.

Now, you already know where I'm going. As I said, homosexuality, a man lying with a man as he would with a woman, is called an abomination. But let's step back a bit.

A lot of what we say about this comes from one book of the Bible, Genesis, and one story, about the four cities, Sodom, Gomorrah, Admah and Zeboiim. So let's refresh our memory.

> "But the men of Sodom were wicked and sinners before the LORD exceedingly." (Genesis 13:13)
>
> "And the LORD said, Because the cry of Sodom and Gomorrah is great, and because their sin is very grievous;" (Genesis 18:20)

Yet God said He would spare their lives, if only 10 righteous people could be found in Sodom (Genesis 18:32).

In Genesis 19:1, two angels came to Sodom. And Lot begged them to come into his house, off the street. In Genesis 19:4, we read:

> "But before they lay down, the men of the city, even the men of Sodom, compassed the house round, both old and young, all the people from every quarter:"

They demanded for Lot to bring out "the men," that they might "know them." When Lot resisted, they threatened to break the door down and do even worse things to Lot than they were going to do to the men! The wicked men of Sodom saw the angels as "fresh meat" to do abominable things to.

And you know the result. God rained fire and brimstone

on Sodom, Gomorrah, Admah and Zeboiim. That once beautiful valley was so well-watered that the Bible says it was like the garden of Eden. Nowadays not even fish or plants can live in the water where those cities once were. That's why it's called "the Dead Sea."

God literally destroyed four cities, their sin was so bad. But believe it or not, after them, the cities of Canaan did many of the same things.

First look at the conclusion of Leviticus 18:26-28:

> "Ye shall therefore keep my statutes and my judgments, and shall not commit any of these abominations; neither any of your own nation, nor any stranger that sojourneth among you: (For all these abominations have the men of the land done, which were before you, and the land is defiled;) That the land spue not you out also, when ye defile it, as it spued out the nations that were before you."

What abominations did the Canaanites do that were so bad God ordered them spat out of the land?

> Uncovering the nakedness of females, old and young, relatives and neighbor's wives. (Leviticus 18:6-20)

> Sacrificing your child to Molech. Some people have likened that, killing your newly-born child, to abortions. (Leviticus 18:21)

> "Thou shalt not lie with mankind, as with womankind: it is abomination." (Leviticus 18:22)

> A person lying with a beast —bestiality. (Leviticus 18:23)

God hates all of these, calling them abominations. He told

the Israelites not to commit any of these abominations, verse 28 again:

> "That the land spue not you out also, when ye defile it, as it spued out the nations that were before you."

There is no doubt that Leviticus 18 lists abominations, things that God hates. But did the men of Sodom really commit abominations? Yes, they were wicked. Yes, four whole cities were destroyed.

But you may hear, and I've heard it many times, "The sin of Sodom was really inhospitality! That's what it says in Ezekiel!"

Let's look at the verse in Ezekiel, and we'll see if they're right, or if what they threatened to do to Lot and the angels was an abomination and really all that bad:

> "Behold, this was the iniquity of thy sister Sodom, pride, fulness of bread, and abundance of idleness was in her and in her daughters [Gomorrah, Admah, and Zeboiim], neither did she strengthen the hand of the poor and needy." (Ezekiel 16:49)

All true! Nobody should have committed sins like that. But that is not what got them destroyed by God. Look at the next verse, which tells what that pride led them to do:

> "And they were haughty, and committed abomination before me: therefore I took them away as I saw good." (Ezekiel 16:50)

So, it wasn't pride that got them "taken away" by destroying their entire civilization. Everyone is guilty of pride. It was what that pride led them to. They had "committed ***abomination*** before God!"

That's why the same abominations in Sodom in Genesis are in Canaan in Leviticus, and it got the Canaanites destroyed. And the Israelites, too, if they committed those same abominable acts.

Today all those abominations make up about half of what is on the internet. From pornography to Ashley Madison, it seems that "everybody is doing it." And some of it has even been made legal to do.

But just because everybody commits an abomination doesn't make it right. And it doesn't matter who is doing it, even God's people. It's still abomination before the Lord. And abominations before God, unlike the purity laws for Israel, never change and apply to everyone.

> "Jesus Christ the same, yesterday, today, and for ever." (Hebrews 13:8)

Just because God's people sin doesn't mean God is happy with it. Sin is sin. And abominations to God, and abominations committed before Him, never change.

It's not a matter of what's abomination to you or me. It's a matter of what's abomination to the Lord.

I hope this has helped make some things clear. Such precision of meaning would be more difficult without the literal words of God.

29

The KJV Is Easier to Understand Than You Think

So many Bible ads over the last 50 years have claimed that the King James Bible is just "too difficult." "They must simplify the words to "make it easy for the common man to understand."

In fact, that belief is part of what fueled the modern Bible translation movement under Eugene Nida. Is the King James Bible really all that difficult?

The King James Bible only has a vocabulary of about 8,000 words. Now, some people will say, "No, that's 12,843." That's because they count in a different way.

Take the word "LOVE:" Love, lovest, loveth. They count that as 3 words, but it's really just one vocabulary word, LOVE.

So in actuality, the King James Bible only has about an 8,000-word vocabulary. 8,000 words is not very much.

Educators know that when a child enters kindergarten he has a vocabulary of about 2,100 words. By the time that child reaches age 6, that "commonly used" vocabulary will go up 500 words to about 2,600. But they will understand 20,000 to 24,000 words. That's up 10 times from the year before. God designed it like that.

So, like I've said since I was a kindergarten teacher, and

studied linguistics, the King James Bible has the vocabulary of a $5^{1/2}$-year-old.

There are about 2,600 proper names and place names in the Bible, over 120 animals to account for, and about 40 terms for weights and measures in the Bible. So that's 2,760 terms that every Bible has to account for. Subtract that from the 8,000 and you get 5,240 words. That's not very many.

Even a child can learn that limited a vocabulary. In fact, my kids learned the Bible at a very early age, starting in Genesis. A number of my viewers on YouTube have told me that they did, too. Even a child with some guidance can learn to read the King James Bible with amazing understanding. And many do.

Some will say, "Yes, they learned vocabulary, but not *those* words." Well, let me tell you a secret. All Bibles have unfamiliar words for you to learn. All that stuff about "simplified vocabulary" is just a lot of advertising hype. We know the kid has the vocabulary, and the ability to learn words at a quick pace.

Could it be that "vocabulary" is not the issue, at all? Could it be that they don't want to appear "old-fashioned," to someone else? They don't want to seem "behind the times"? Could they be seeking the approval of men?

Let me get this straight. New Bibles are changing or missing hundreds of words, phrases and verses —and they're upset over a little Thee and Thou? Give me a break. Which is more important: to have man's approval? Or the pure words of the Living God in your language?

Think about that the next time somebody offers you a "new and improved," or a "simplified" Bible.

30

It Keeps Jesus Sinless

According to a recent Barna survey, 44% of Americans surveyed said that they think Jesus was not God. When Barna asked them if they believed Jesus sinned, I would expect that the 44% would say "yes."

But wait. According to the numbers, 52% said that they agreed that Jesus sinned as a human. Okay, the 44% I understand. If He's not God, then of course He was a sinful human.

But what about the other 8%?

I checked my numbers. That 8% comes from the number that believed that Jesus was God! So they believe that Jesus was God, and that He sinned as a human.

What's wrong with this picture?

8% of these people are in a very confusing position. Sinning is disobeying God. They believe Jesus was God. Yet they believe Jesus sinned.

So, God disobeyed God? It doesn't make any sense!

Could their Bibles have had something to do with it? Walk through this with me.

First, in Chapter 1 of ***Look What's Missing***, I tell about one missing word that made Jesus a liar. In John 7:8 Jesus was asked by His brothers if He was going down to Jerusalem to the required feast.

And He said these words in the King James:

> "Go ye up unto this feast: I go not up yet unto this feast; for my time is not yet full come."

Two verses later, when His brethren had gone up to Jerusalem, it says:

> "then went he also up unto the feast, not openly, but as it were in secret."

That's all well and good.

But in 21 Bibles, many of which are in churches today, the new NIV, the ESV, the New American Standard, they take out that crucial word "YET." That makes Jesus say, "I am not going up to this feast." And we know that is a lie.

That would make Jesus a liar. It only takes one lie to make Jesus a liar. But it also makes Jesus a sinner. Wait. Jesus said, "I am the way, the truth, and the life:" (John 14:6). Now He cannot be the *Truth* and tell a lie. Not even once.

But these 21 Bibles make Jesus into a liar. That's one example.

Second, in Matthew 5:22, Jesus said (again, I am quoting our Lord):

> "But I say unto you, That whosoever is angry with his brother without a cause shall be in danger of the judgment..."

So being angry "with a cause" is fine. It's being angry "without a cause" that makes God upset.

What about Jesus? Two times in His ministry Jesus cleansed the temple. He purged the temple, in fact, and He chased the money changers out of the temple!

Jesus didn't have an intellectual discussion. He didn't sit

down and say, "Please stop doing that. This is my Father's house." No! Take a look at John 2:15-16, this is just one example:

> "And when he had made a scourge of small cords, he drove them all out of the temple and the sheep, and the oxen; and poured out the changers' money, and overthrew the tables; And said unto them that sold doves, Take these things hence; make not my Father's house an house of merchandise."

Jesus was angry. And He had every right to be! It was "with cause."

But take a look at the Big List on page 197 of ***Look What's Missing***. At least 36 modern Bibles remove those words "without a cause," making Jesus a sinner —three times![11] The NIV, the ESV, the NAS, the New Living and 32 others, have Jesus as a sinner at least twice and 21 of them a liar once!

Again, these are used in modern churches and in people's homes, today.

So let me ask you a question. Most modern Bibles, like the NIV or ESV, have Jesus at least twice, maybe three times, as a sinner. How long is it until these Bible readers, even if they believe Jesus was God, but they believe Jesus was a sinner, start also believing that Jesus wasn't divine, after all?

There are two kinds of Bibles: There's a "sinful Jesus Bible" which is most of the ones on the market today, and a "sinless Jesus Bible."

Now if you are leading a person to Christ, and you want them to come to a sinless Christ, do you want to give them

---

11) See Mark 3:5 where Jesus is specifically said to look "round about on them with anger."

a "sinful Christ Bible," or a "sinless Christ Bible"?

Remember, these eight percenters, they are people in transition. They don't stay in a contradictory place for long. If these 8% of Americans believe that Jesus was a sinner, how long till they stop believing Jesus was God?

31

Its Doubters Aren't Sure What They Believe

It's ironic.

People seem to love to belittle others who believe that the King James Bible is God's preserved words in English and trust it. But they're not even sure what they believe.

You want proof? "You King James Only people are all alike!" How many times have you heard it, read it, or had it said to you? They even have an abbreviation for it: KJVO. They treat it like it's a virus.

They ridicule it. They push it away. They're afraid they might catch it! How dare we trust something that's infallibly true! How dare we trust it above our own preferences, our own opinions, our own professors and preachers! How dare we judge others by an infallible standard!

Beyond all the hype, it's simple. God promised (and God's promises mean something) to preserve His words. Jesus said, "Heaven and earth shall pass away, but my words shall not pass away."

If they "shall not pass away," then they're still here. That means we can *find* them. And we believe we *have* them. We believe that God preserved His words through His faithful followers and that those words and the correct translation of them are the KJV.

Why is that so threatening? "Well... you BELIEVE IT!"
Yes, we do.

"Well, you.... base your thoughts and your aspirations and your hopes and your beliefs and your morals on it!"
Yes, we do.

"Well, it's wrong! You've got to look at MY version!!"
Why?

Brothers and sisters, this is the point. Why should we, who believe the King James, have to look at any modern version? If someone tells you you've got to believe their modern version, ask *them* a question: Do you believe every word, every phrase, every sentence, every chapter, every book of your Bible?

"Pretty much."

Oh, so you aren't even sure what **you** believe, but you are angry at me because I believe I have God's words?

"But my Bible is 95% correct!!" (...or 99% correct —whatever)

Great! You show me which 95% I can believe, and then which 5% I can throw out!

See, they have a Bible that's 95% the same as the King James, and since they started using them, something started happening. They started openly questioning basic doctrines, like whether Christ is God and eternal, the existence of heaven and hell, the existence of angels and devils, whether you must do works to *be* saved, whether you must do works to *stay* saved, important doctrines like that.

You know, maybe that 5% difference, adding to and taking away from God's words, was... BAD.

And the Devil's just laughin' and scratchin' and pattin' himself on the back! He's got so many people doubting

God's words, with just 5% or 1% difference! It didn't take much, did it?

The bottom line: it's hypocrisy to lay into those who believe that God preserved His words and believe those words —when you don't trust yours.

And what's wrong with that, anyway?

Great men of God have trusted these words for the last 400 years!

We KJV-Only people are alike in this; we all believe that God's words are more important than our own opinions. And we are all *unwilling* to change God's words, to suit our own opinions.

How about you?

32

It Tells You What Its Doubters Don't Want to Believe

I understand that some people are making fun of my videos and the things I have said in my books.

I understand. They have every right to feel threatened by what is being said. I used to be in the same, uncomfortable position that they are. They would have to believe some pretty big things.

Would you like a list?

When I hold in my hands a Book that I believe and base my Christian faith on, some Christians don't believe that. I sympathize with them. It puts them in an uncomfortable position.

They'd have to believe that the God who created the universe out of nothing and holds it in the palm of His hand, who sustains it until He decides to reform it or recreate it, who gives us the very air that we breathe, kept His promise to preserve His words and put it in a Book for us to read and believe.

They'd have to believe that the God who created and sustains the universe will also judge all people and left His instructions so you know what you can and must not do. They'd have to believe that God didn't hide His words for century after century, only to be found by or searched out by non-believers.

They'd have to believe that God, who created and sustains

the universe, who also promised "Heaven and earth shall pass away, but my words shall not pass away" and recorded it three times, kept His promise and preserved His words in a Book for us to read and believe.

They'd have to believe that we will all be held accountable to those words. They'd have to believe that He will rightly find us guilty if we add to or take away a word from them.

Then they'd have to pattern all their doctrines, all their beliefs, all their theological speculations, in such a way that they do not change the words that are already in this Book.

And they'd have to believe that the minute their theology differs from the words of this Book, it is their theology that is wrong, not the Book.

I understand. They may have lots of reasons not to believe. And they can devise in their hearts all sorts of other reasons and theories against it, and objections to it, all that their heart desires.

But Jeremiah 17:9 says:

> "The heart is deceitful above all things, and desperately wicked: who can know it?"

I trust God. I do not trust myself above God. And I am willing to have my life tried by the words of this Book, the King James Bible, and no other.

No fair for them to change the words by appealing to the Greek. This is the accurate translation of the Greek, the Hebrew and any other languages that are translated in this Book.

I understand. It is very limiting. But it is also very freeing. Think about it.

I am free to trust God and to *know* what He thinks about a myriad of topics, without question. I am not beholden to pastor, or church, or king, or priest, or pope. I am beholden only to God, through the words in this Book.

I get to bypass all that. But they can object if they have to. I objected for years, saying "The only thing worse than the King James Bible is the Living Bible." And then I had to eat my words.

They can ridicule if they must. I ridiculed for years. But I sincerely hope they keep on looking. Because if they are honest, they will find what I found. God *did* keep His promise. God *did* preserve His words.

And He did put them in English in a Book that we can read and believe.

And they are here for us right now in the King James Bible.

Here I stand.

33

A Few Tiny Changes Make a Big Difference

Recently I heard a sermon by a young man, whom I am sure was or had recently been a Bible college student. I am sure this man had a heart for the Lord. He wanted to serve Him, and do things that pleased His God. Of that I have no doubt.

But at the same time, he did the same thing as I did in Bible college. He trusted his professors. And that is what led him to make a few simple mistakes.

Mistake #1: Basing the sermon on a word that is not in the text he was using. This sermon was on the importance of fellowship in the gospel, a wonderful topic. And it was right here, in my King James Bible:

> "Always in every prayer of mine for you all making request with joy, For your fellowship in the gospel from the first day until now;" (Philippians 1:4-5)

However, his Bible of choice, the ESV (English Standard Version) does not have the word "fellowship" in the text at all. It says "...because of your partnership in the gospel..."

Okay, wait a minute. Fellowship and partnership are not the same thing. Fellowship is companionship. It's a closeness term. It is an equality and a friendship term. But partnership is a business term. It makes the gospel work sound like a business firm.

So "gospel fellowship" sounds great —which is why it was a good title. But their Bible said "gospel partnership" which sounds more like having a job than having companions. But more than that, the King James is right. "Fellowship," κοινωνία (*koinonia*), is what it is all about, not a mere "partnership."

Mistake #2: Teaching people to doubt the Bible that is in their hands. This is important. If you're going to teach the Bible, and what you are teaching makes them doubt the Bible, something, somewhere, is wrong.

In this case it was the Greek word δοῦλος (*doulos*) in Philippians 1:1 (and other verses that he listed). Now the King James correctly translates the word as "servant."

But this young preacher did what every one of us Greek students was taught to do in Bible college. He said "servant" was wrong. It should be "slave."

We are "slaves" to Jesus Christ? But that is not true. The King James again is correct.

What is a "servant"? It is one who serves. There are two kinds of service: voluntary or involuntary. And there were different forms of service in the first century: there were people who were in voluntary servitude to pay off a debt (the Bible has a 7-year limit on that). There were people who were servants, like we are employees. That's why we can use those verses for us, now.

And there were the slaves, captured in war, who had no will, no choice of their own, but were subject to the whim of their captors.

Well, wouldn't you know? That Greek word *doulos* means

the same thing as our English word, "servant," depending on how it is used. So, the best translation is "servant," like the King James, not "slave," like the Jehovah's Witness Bible and many others.

But in fact, even the ESV he was holding had it right! It said "servant," just like the King James. But his professors convinced him that it should say "slave." So, he spent the next five minutes telling everyone how they could not believe the Bible they were holding in their hands.

He may not have known it, but he was basically telling them they can't trust any Bible. Instead, we need those "doubting Thomas" scholars.

Let me show you how I know the King James is right, exactly as it is!

Look at Galatians 5:13:

> "For, brethren, ye have been called unto liberty; only use not liberty for an occasion to the flesh, but by love *serve* one another."

That word "serve" is the verb form of that same Greek word *doulos*!

We are at liberty, set free from bondage to sin by the sacrifice of Christ! We are not slaves any longer. As the Bible says:

> "Stand fast therefore in the liberty wherewith Christ hath made us free, and be *not* entangled again with the yoke of bondage." (Galatians 5:1)

Slavery?

We are not *slaves*. We are not under bondage. We are free! But we get to *serve* one another, as we serve our heavenly Father!

Now that's what I'd preach, so you would walk away from the sermon clenching your King James Bible in your hands, saying, "Wow! My King James Bible was right all along!"

And you'd walk away from church with even more faith in every word of God's preserved words in English, the King James Bible.

But when this man preached, as we all were taught to do, the people walked out, with less faith in any Bible, much less the one in their hands. And I can imagine them saying something like this:

"I've heard a lot of sermons in my day, and this was definitely one of them... what's for lunch?"

Don't make the mistakes we did.

34

It Destroys Inaccurate Bible Memes

Did you know that God says "fear not" 365 times in the Bible —the same as the number of days in the year?

Neither did I! That's because it's patently false! Lloyd John Ogilvie, the former Chaplain of the U.S. Senate, wrote in Facing the Future without Fear (1999), p. 22, "The Lord's constant word to us is 'fear not!' There are 366 'fear not!' verses in the Bible —one for every day of the year and an extra one for leap year!"

That sounds good. It preaches well —but it's completely wrong! Want to know the real numbers?

I got home from work and saw this "meme" on Facebook, the picture with the words on it, and it told about these 365 "fear nots."

I decided to check it out for myself. This is what I do to relax. I'm a wonk. But a Bible-believing one!

It turns out that the King James actually says, "don't be afraid" in two ways: "Fear not" and "Be not afraid." "Fear not" is stated 63 times in 63 verses. But it is not stated by God, or else it is not a godly command to "fear not," in 24 of those verses.

That means God or His representative commands us to "Fear not" a total of 39 times. That's the same number as the number of books in the Old Testament. "Be not afraid" is found 28 times in 26 verses.

But in one of those verses it is not stated by God, or not a godly command to "fear not." That means God or His representative commands us "Be not afraid" a total of 27 times.

That's the same number of times as there are books in the New Testament. 39 and 27. A total of 66 times it says "fear not" in the Bible. See the picture?

I think the whole 365-366 thing happened because of a mistake! Here's what I think happened. Some enterprising Bible-believer did the research and found the truth.

Then he preached the truth. And then someone in his congregation thought, "I don't need to take notes. I can remember it." But he didn't.

He got home that night and he said, "Now what was that number again? The number of days in the week? No. Seven is too few. The number of chapters in the Bible? No, that's 1,189. It's too many. The number of days in a year! 365! That must be it!"

So, when he preached, he simply said, "365 Fear nots!" And somebody took notes. And then those guys preached, saying "365 Fear nots!"

And others wrote down notes. And eventually it came down to Lloyd John Ogilvie who heard it, wrote it down, and put it in a book, and everybody's been quoting it for decades, from that day to this, right up to that Facebook meme last night.

And over the decades, no one took the time to just look it up? Wow. One person online tried all sorts of different versions to try and come up with 365. They found the 365 was wrong but had no idea what was right. It's a memorable number, right? But we have to remember the right numbers!

That's why God gave us the right Bible, His preserved

words in English, the King James Bible, a Bible that is beyond dispute, our final authority.

Then we take the numbers from here, and from nobody and nowhere else. Like I did. Maybe now people will start quoting the right numbers!

It's still totally cool: 39x for "fear not" and 27x for "be not afraid," just like the 39 books of the Old Testament and 27 books of the New Testament. It's easy to remember, isn't it now?

It's amazing what we can do, when we have our pocket King James Bible, even our pocket concordance, to find out what God has said. So, let me ask you:

What's in YOUR pocket?

35

The OAO Doctrine Was Created to Reject It

It's amazing what you can learn when you put events and people on a timeline.

Which came first: the chicken or the egg?

If you believe in Creation by God, as stated in the Bible, you already know the answer. The chicken was created first, with the capacity to mate and make eggs.

Which came first: the Original Autographs Only doctrine, or the "King James Only" doctrine, or its formal name, "Providential Preservation"? The answer is in the timeline!

The Westminster Confession of Faith was written over 370 years ago in 1646. It has been the standard statement of doctrine of the Church of England and became the basis of other statements of faith, including the London Baptist Confession of 1689.

Providential Preservation wasn't a new doctrine even then. It was a very ancient and Bible-believing doctrine. They just wrote it down for all to see in 1646. Take a look at it for yourself online. It's just filled with scriptures to back up each point.

Chapter One is called "Of the Holy Scripture." Let me summarize and cut it down —a lot.

Part 1 says that nature shows God's goodness, wisdom

and power. But it's not sufficient to know God and His will regarding salvation.

So first, God spoke to the church. Then He inspired them: "to commit the same wholly unto writing: which maketh the Holy Scripture to be most necessary..." That is why we need and have the Bible, to preserve God's words to get us saved and protected from the Devil's deceit.

Part 2 lists only the 66 books of our present Bible as the scriptures.

Part 3 is about the Apocrypha. It's so short, you've got to hear it:

> "The books commonly called Apocrypha, not being of divine inspiration, are no part of the canon of the Scripture, and therefore are of no authority in the church of God, nor to be any otherwise approved, or made use of, than other human writings."

That is very well said —in 1646!

Now let me jump to Part 8. Again, I'll radically shorten it.

> "The Old Testament in Hebrew ... and the New Testament in Greek ... being immediately [as it was being written] inspired by God, and, by his singular care and providence, kept pure in all ages, are therefore authentical; so as, ... the church is finally to appeal unto them."

This means God provided ("providence") for the Church by keeping His words pure ("preservation"). That's not natural. God supernaturally preserved His words.

Here is a quote by Gleason Archer, "A Survey of Old Testament Introduction, Revised and Expanded," page 25: "...it would take nothing short of a miracle to insure the inerrancy of a copy of an original manuscript."

Exactly! We have a supernatural, miraculous, Bible! Anything short of that is just a book.

It goes on,

> "But, because these original tongues are not known to all the people of God ... therefore they are to be translated into the vulgar [common] language of every nation unto which they come, that ... they ... through patience and comfort of the Scriptures, may have hope."

Note that those translations are called scriptures. And you can see for yourself, it's all backed up by scripture verses.

This was written when? In 1646, summarizing what scriptures and Bible believers had believed for centuries. But in the 1800s, everything changed.

In 1810 a Catholic priest, Johann Leonhard Hug, put out a little, 28-page book in Latin only, declaring that Codex Vaticanus was actually from the 300s AD. It's called "De antiquitate Codicis Vaticani commentatio" *(Study Concerning the Antiquity of Codex Vaticanus).*

Scholars bought it, hook, line and thinker. Suddenly paleographers and text critics wanted to see the Vaticanus. But the Vatican kept it under lock and key, under the protection of the Jesuit Cardinal Angelo Mai. Vaticanus, a document that magically showed up in the Vatican Library in 1475, was now sought after by Protestants, to replace their preserved Bible!

But it was only one book. Text scholars knew there was nothing to compare it to. They needed another text before they could justify changing the Bible.

Then poof! In 1843 Constantin Tischendorf, after

speaking with Pope Leo XIII and Jesuit Cardinal Mai, started raising funds. When he had raised enough money, in 1844 Tischendorf made a beeline for Cairo to get permission, then 275 miles across desert to St. Catherine's monastery, where he "just happened to find" —exactly what all the scholars were looking for at that time— a second supposedly ancient Greek Bible! Imagine that!

(At this time it was still white, by the way.) He stole 43 sheets and returned to Saxony. This became the Codex Friderico-Augustanus.

By 1859, with the help of the Russian government, Tischendorf got the book, which he called "Codex Sinaiticus" or "Aleph," out of St. Catherine's monastery, to Cairo, then to Russia.

But the remaining pages are now darkened. Then he published typeset facsimiles, starting in 1862.

After 2 unsuccessful visits to the Vatican, finally the pope gave Tischendorf the privilege of checking over the Codex Vaticanus, which he published as a typeset facsimile in 1867.

Now there were two codices for the paleographers to fight over.

And that was what Brooke Foss Westcott and Fenton John Anthony Hort were waiting for! From that time, Hort started working fervently on a new theory, that wherever Sinaiticus and Vaticanus agreed, either to add words or to take away words, that would become their "new" Greek text.

There were two Convocations, deciding bodies, for the Church of England, the smaller Northern Convocation in York and the larger Southern Convocation in Canterbury. Westcott and Hort had to have permission to make a committee to revise the English Bible. The Northern Convocation said No. But on February 10, 1870, the Southern Convocation said Yes.

Once the Committee was at their task, the members were secretly given this changed text of Westcott and Hort, largely based upon the Sinaiticus and Vaticanus. They made their Revised Version based on that radically changed text, not on the traditional preserved texts of the Bible.

That brings us to 1881. By August they had planned to unveil their new "Revised Version" of the English Bible.

But what about all those changes? Their Confession of Faith said that God providentially preserved the words of their English Bible. But now they were going to take away words, phrases and whole verses and change words. And they based this on a newly-discovered text from a desert monastery and another text hidden under lock and key by the Vatican. It was not based on the Bibles handed down by faithful, persecuted believers.

For 235 years the Westminster Confession of Faith had stood. But before August of 1881, they needed a change of doctrine, before the English Revised Version hit the bookstores.

Get this: just four months before that, in April of 1881, two Princeton professors went to work to change the Westminster Confession regarding preservation. These two were Principal of Princeton Seminary, Archibald Alexander Hodge and professor of Theology, Benjamin Breckinridge Warfield.

They modified the doctrine of inspiration and preservation! Look at this: "We do not assert that the common text, but only that the original autographic text WAS [past tense] inspired." Instead of openly rejecting the statement of faith, they changed the statement of faith!

So when, four months later, Westcott and Hort's gutted New Testament hit the shelves, they could feel theologically justified in rejecting the King James Bible.

Now in churches all over the world, people think that OAO, Original Autographs Only, is the original doctrine!

Once again:

Providential Preservation, 371 years old.

Original Autographs Only, just 136 years old.

It's a doctrine no older than the English Revised Version itself. That's no coincidence. It's perfect timing.

Original Autographs Only was a doctrine made up to support Westcott and Hort, Tischendorf and Tregelles, and the brand-new Bible based on the Sinaiticus and the Vaticanus. That's where the modern doctrine came from. That's where the modern Bibles come from.

We base our faith on a promise by God.

They base their faith on a doubt.

We trust God's ability to keep His promises.

They doubt God and trust text critics to tell them which texts they can believe —or not.

It's called the Christian faith —not the Christian doubt.

We are willing to place 100% faith in God's book.

They are *un*willing to place 100% faith in anything.

Chicken or the egg? Providential Preservation or Original Autographs Only? Which came first?

For Bible believers, the chicken came first.

And historically, Providential Preservation, and King James Only, came first.

Original Autographs Only isn't a statement of faith at all. It's a statement of doubt.

Take your pick!

Trust God and get His Book,

Or trust the scholars and get —basically nothing but doubt.

36

It Exposes Confused Teachers

You're listening to two Bible teachers. Each one claims he is teaching the Bible. But they totally disagree. How can you tell if someone is really teaching the Bible?

Does he switch from the King James Bible to another version in order to prove his point? Red flag! Does he switch to what he claims to be the Greek or Hebrew meaning, in order to prove a point that is not clear in the text itself already? Red flag!

Does he claim: "The King James is translated wrong here," when it disagrees with his personal teaching? Red flag! Does he completely disregard the regular meaning in favor of a spiritualized one, without ever showing how that's justified, to leave the literal meaning of the text itself? Red flag! Or does he simply summarize Bible teachings and never get around to actually reading the scripture itself? Red flag!

The rule is simple. If the plain sense makes sense, don't seek another sense.

May I give you a quick example? In Luke 10 is the story that is called The Good Samaritan. For 32 years I've been taught that the priest and the Levite didn't help the poor man who was wounded because they didn't want to soil themselves and become unclean to perform their Temple obligations in Jerusalem.

Is that what the text says? Let's check. Luke 10:30, "And Jesus answering said, A certain man went down from Jerusalem to Jericho and fell among thieves..." He went what? Up or down? Down. Directions in the Bible are to be taken literally.

Jerusalem is over 2,500 feet above sea level, and Jericho is 820 feet below sea level. You have to go down 3,400 feet from the one to the other. Verse 31 says "And by chance there came down a certain priest that way..."

Verse 32 says, "And *likewise* a Levite..." They weren't going *up* to Jerusalem. They were going *down* to Jericho. In other words, both the priest and the Levite had fulfilled their Temple obligations. They didn't have to worry about being unclean to do them and had *no excuse* for not helping that half-dead, wounded man.

Look what you need. You need *what* God said, the *way* God said it, *word* for *word*, with the *meaning* that God intended. That's called "Formal Equivalence." You need God's words, preserved through history, by faithful men, using Formal Equivalence, in the King James Bible. Don't accept anything less.

That's how you can tell if a person's really, at least, attempting to teach from the Bible.

37

It Carries the Same Inspiration as the Originals

Someone issued me a challenge yesterday. He said, "Can a translation be inspired? Show me, using only the Bible for your answer."

Actually, that's a fascinating question.

I'm about to show you how a translation can both 1) be inspired, and 2) carry the original inspiration, even into a third language.

First, what is "inspiration"?

I can hear the college students and Bible church members saying it, "God-breathed," in Greek, θεόπνευστος (*theopneustos*).

Yes, "God breathed." But God breathed where?

Inspiration Type One: God put His breath into a person.

> "And the LORD God formed man of the dust of the ground, and breathed into his nostrils the breath of life; and man became a living soul." (Genesis 2:7)

God breathed into Adam's nostrils, and he received the breath of life. And with that breath of life in that body, man became a living soul.

So that inspiration literally gave Adam life. That's Inspiration Type One.

Inspiration Type Two is God speaking His own words through a person. That shows up either in what the person says, or in what the person writes. This scripture states it in God's words:

> "For the prophecy came not in old time by the will of man: but holy men of God spake as they were moved by the Holy Ghost." (2 Peter 1:21)

Let's take that apart. The prophecy did not come by the will of man. So it was by no means man's idea. That means it was God's idea.

Then it says, "holy men of God" —that is, men dedicated wholly to God, for God's own purposes— "spake as they were moved by the Holy Ghost."

Who's the mover? Not the man. The mover is the Holy Ghost, God. The Holy Ghost moved the men. Those men, not against their will, but in line with their will, spoke God's words God's way. That was called "prophecy."

Inspiration is God moving a person to say or write what He wants, the way He wills, not the way man wants.

So, is the Old Testament inspired? You can look up the 52 times "scripture" or "scriptures" is used in the New Testament. It covers the Old Testament Law, Prophets, and Writings. It's all inspired scripture.

Follow with me.

The Old Testament is scripture.

So are the things God said and God wrote through Paul. The apostle Peter wrote by inspiration:

> "And account that the longsuffering of our Lord is salvation; even as our beloved brother Paul also according to the wisdom given unto him hath written

unto you; As also in all his epistles, speaking in them of these things; in which are some things hard to be understood, which they that are unlearned and unstable wrest, as they do also the other scriptures, unto their own destruction." (2 Peter 3:15-16)

Hear those words, "Paul also according to the wisdom given unto him hath written unto you…"

God gave the wisdom to Paul. And Paul wrote it down.

And people who wrest, twist, wrestle, Paul's writings are actually wresting "scriptures." And they are scriptures like the "other scriptures."

So the Old Testament is inspired. The words of Paul are inspired. Then Paul quoted Jesus, in 1 Timothy 5:18, when he said ἄξιος ὁ ἐργάτης τοῦ μισθοῦ αὐτοῦ (axios ho ergatēs tou misthou autou), quoting Jesus' words from the Gospel of Luke! (Luke 10:7, "…the labourer is worthy of his hire")

Luke is also inspired. We could go on. You can see how scripture is inspired, the Old and New Testaments, as we have them, all 66 books. God spoke through the authors.

Look up all 52 places "scripture" or "scriptures" appears. You will be amazed at what you learn that God calls scripture.

There are three divisions of the Old Testament. They are called the Law, the Prophets and the Psalms or the Writings. All three are widely quoted in the New Testament.

The Psalms, like Psalm 118 quoted in Matthew 21:42:

> "Jesus saith unto them, Did ye never read in the scriptures, The stone which the builders rejected, the same is become the head of the corner: this is the Lord's doing, and it is marvellous in our eyes?"

The Prophets, like Isaiah 61 quoted in Luke 4:18-19. In

verse 21 Jesus said,

> "This day is this scripture fulfilled in your ears."

And of course, **the Law**, as in Genesis through Deuteronomy. John cited Exodus 12:46 in John 19:36:

> "For these things were done, that the scripture should be fulfilled, A bone of him shall not be broken."

Jesus was the Passover Lamb.
And Paul cited Genesis 15:6 in Romans 4:3:

> "For what saith the scripture? Abraham believed God, and it was counted unto him for righteousness."

And in case that wasn't enough, Jesus summed it up Himself, in Luke 24:44-45:

> "And he said unto them, These are the words which I spake unto you, while I was yet with you, that all things must be fulfilled, which were written in the law of Moses, and in the prophets, and in the psalms, concerning me. Then opened he their understanding, that they might understand the scriptures,"

As I said, it's a fascinating study.
But let's take it a step further.

Type 1: God breathed life into Adam and made him a living soul.

Type 2: God breathed His words by the Holy Ghost into certain people, not spoken or written by their will, but by God's will.

Does that include translations?

Consider Exodus 1:22:

> "And Pharaoh charged all his people, saying, Every son that is born ye shall cast into the river, and every daughter ye shall save alive."

Did Pharaoh speak Hebrew? Not to his people, he didn't. He spoke Egyptian. And yet was this written in the scriptures in Egyptian? No, it was translated into Hebrew. So, the Hebrew was an inspired translation of the Egyptian.

Daniel 3:24:

> "Then Nebuchadnezzar the king was astonied, and rose up in haste, and spake, and said unto his counsellers, Did not we cast three men bound into the midst of the fire? They answered and said unto the king, True, O king."

Did Nebuchadnezzar and his counselors speak Hebrew? Not to each other. They spoke Babylonian. And the scripture's Hebrew (or Aramaic, Syrian) was an inspired translation of the Babylonian.

What language did the King of Syria speak? Big hint: it wasn't Hebrew. 1 Kings 20:23:

> "And the servants of the king of Syria said unto him, Their gods are gods of the hills; therefore, they were stronger than we; but let us fight against them in the plain, and surely we shall be stronger than they."

They spoke Syrian, or Aramaic, and we have an inspired translation of their words into the Hebrew, right here in the scriptures!

One more. Look at Paul's words in Acts 22:1-2:

> "Men, brethren, and fathers, hear ye my defence

It Carries the Same Inspiration as the Originals

which I make now unto you. (And when they heard that he spake in the Hebrew tongue to them, they kept the more silence...)"

It's no secret to us that Paul spoke Hebrew. But wait. What language was that written down in? That's right. Greek. So, the Greek is an inspired translation of Paul the apostle's words in Hebrew.

In fact, the scriptures are filled with translations, and they are inspired translations!

God promises that His words will be preserved, even though heaven and earth pass away. God promises that those words are pure, so they have no error.

But I hear the objectors: No! It says in all my theology books that there can be no completely accurate translation into another language. Something is always lost!

Then those theology books are saying that God was in error, because God kept on putting inspired translations into the scriptures themselves.

Even Pontius Pilate's wife, her Latin words are translated into the Greek scriptures in Matthew 27:19:

> "Have thou nothing to do with that just man: for I have suffered many things this day in a dream because of him."

If you have an accurate translation, you have lost nothing. So, if you have an accurate translation of the inspired scriptures, you have also lost nothing. You now have the inspired scriptures in a new language.

And if you have translated accurately, then that translation is not "re-inspired" or "double inspiration." It simply carries that inspiration into a new language.

Did you ever wonder why God revealed the Old Testament in Hebrew, but the New Testament in Greek? God is interested in translating His inspired words into all the languages of earth.

Just remember, holding in your hands the King James Bible, a fully accurate translation of God's holy words of Greek and Hebrew, you have the inspired words of God in your language. They carry that same inspiration, since they have not added to nor taken away from what God said.

38

It Exposes the Real Know-It-Alls

Does anything bug you as much as a "know-it-all"?

A know-it-all is completely different from an expert. But how can you tell which is which?

An expert studies his craft carefully, for years practicing to get better, and after many years is able to state his conclusions, or opinions, or theories. And we tend to trust experts because we know that they have spent years working at all of that.

But a know-it-all is none of that. A know-it-all is often a drop-out from a college or course or program. He's "much too smart for them."

A know-it-all has theories without research, conclusions without study, answers without preparation. And a know-it-all expects to be believed, because....

Actually, I don't know why they expect to be believed.

They just do. And maybe that's why they change their minds so much. They didn't really have a solid basis for what they believed, so it was no big thing if they changed it.

That is so much like Bible versions!

King James Bible believers are vilified, because they say, "Thus saith the Lord!" And at first glance, maybe their critics are right.

They pick up a Bible, the King James Bible, and they say,

"Thus saith the Lord!" and believe every word of it. They ignore the modern critics and their web pages and their books and their articles in *Christianity Today*.

They don't listen to the experts who have been teaching against the King James for decades. They just believe the Book. It's their Book. And they will accept no other.

They do certainly sound like know-it-alls, don't they?

But wait. Maybe there is another way to look at this. The King James Bible came from texts preserved and passed down over thousands of years, many times at the cost of their owners' lives.

The King James Bible was prepared with the help and consent of Bible-believers who were scholars.

Over 400 years tested.

Over 400 years proved.

Over 400 years believed, and as a result, we have over 400 years of success stories, including the largest missionary movement for God in history, by people of faith.

Modern versions are changing the meaning of historically-understood words: "disbelieve" to "disobey;" "are saved" to "are being saved;" "only begotten" to "only" or "unique;" Jesus as "Son" to merely God's "Servant."

Modern versions are based mainly on two corrupt manuscripts that removed and changed hundreds of words, and phrases, and verses. And yet all the versions and even their scholars disagree about which words phrases, and verses should be removed or changed! That's why there's always a new one!

I think the real know-it-alls are the ones with the nerve to change God's preserved, inspired, holy, tested words —approved by people of faith.

It Exposes the Real Know-It-Alls

That's why the King James Bible believer can preach with faith, and say, "Thus saith the Lord!" with all the fire that the Holy Ghost puts inside them.

Because you know what? It's just not so easy to get all fired up about "The opinion of the majority of the scholars at the moment is…!"

And nobody likes a "know-it-all."

39

It's a Source of Godly Zeal

I want to give you a bit of a "feel for my zeal."

I am indebted to a man I've never met. If it weren't for him, I wouldn't have seen that mule-choking King James Bible at the United Church of Religious Science on Palm Canyon Drive in Palm Springs, back in 1979.

That was where I saw the beautiful white Bible, with the enticing words, "Family Tree" on the box. It was, as my Grandpa would say, "big enough to choke a mule." The letters were plenty large, and there was a center column with definitions of some words I might not understand and some cross-references.

There were also helps such as a dictionary in the back, how to lead someone to Christ, and some Bible maps.

And of course, there was room for writing my family tree, something the Daniels family has always loved. We had an 1800s family Bible from the South, and it told a lot of history, but this was brand-new, with lots of room. How could I resist this Bible?

When the Lord brought me back to Himself on August 24, 1980, it was to that Bible I ran, to find out where I had heard those words the Lord spoke into my heart. And there it was: Matthew 7:21-23. So convicting!

I prayed to receive the Lord on June 7, 1972. But I formally met my Saviour and my heavenly Father that night, through that Bible. I will never forget it.

And I will never regret spending the $30.00 for that Bible. It was the most I'd ever spent on a book. And it was worth every penny.

That was the biggest book I had ever carried with me, and one of the biggest Bibles I had ever seen. But I was not embarrassed to carry it around. I hadn't a care about what people thought of me. I carried books all the time, everywhere, for years. But this was the biggest of all. And this was The Book. It doesn't get better than this.

God blessed those first few days of seeking God and hearing through His words in a special way. I was all alone with my heavenly Father in the beautiful Southern California desert.

I loved living in the desert, both day and night. While the days could get up above 105°F or even hotter, I never really felt it. It was very dry and comfortable. About 3:00pm every day a pleasant wind would blow into Sky Valley from the west, giving respite from the heat, if it had gotten to be too much, although it almost never did.

Nearly every night I could look up and see the Milky Way clearly, along with other stars and planets. When Mars was up, it actually shone with a strong reddish color.

Growing up in a suburb of Los Angeles, I had never seen color in heavenly bodies before through the smog and electric lights. But now it was an almost-nightly privilege. I was directly south of one of my favorite camping spots, Joshua Tree National Monument, and directly north of a hilly section that is the actual main line of the San Andreas Fault.

And I was directly next door to —nobody! The closest

person, when someone visited his property, was acres away.

I could walk around the desert, even when the moon wasn't shining, and see my way around by the stars, without a flashlight. Actually, using a flashlight blinded me to the rest of the desert, save the small area illuminated in front of me. It was far safer to go by the stars and the moon, if it was out.

I loved the desert. It was like camping every day. When it was warm at night (which was quite often), I loved to take my bed roll, consisting of a polyethylene foam mattress, sheets, cover and pillow, up to the roof of the 12" x 16" squatter's shack we called home. I could sit or lay and watch the stars and planets move around me —or rather, around Polaris, the North Star.

And though it was late August, I had no qualms about reading scripture and seeking God, on the desert floor by day or on my roof by night.

By day I just sat down by the cholla (CHOY-uh) and barrel cactus plants and prayed as a friend had instructed me when I was still into the occult.

I prayed something like this. "Father, in the name of Your Son, please let the Holy Spirit reveal to me the scriptures." And I began in Genesis and Matthew, Old and New Testaments. That's it.

I had no fancy commentary series, knew no Christians to help me understand, and certainly trusted none of my occultic friends to help. I was on new ground, holy ground.

I was left to rely on my heavenly Father to help me understand as I read. I asked Him the answer when I didn't understand the meaning of words. And I trusted Him that He knew, even though I didn't, He knew the answer to every question.

It was two years later, in Bible college one morning, a word was clearly defined in class, exactly the way the Lord put in my heart when I had prayed to Him in August of 1980. I smiled and quietly said, "Wow, God! You knew what You were talking about!"

(I think my wife Debbie remembers that day.)

By night I had "talks" with God, telling Him all about my life and reasoning out loud about His holy words.

One evening "talk" went something like this: "Father, I was told when I was young that a committee got together and decided the text that they wanted in the Bible and put that in. Then they decided the words they wanted out of the Bible and left that out. But I don't believe that.

Father, I believe You are big enough to superintend the text of the Bible, so that what You wanted to be in is in, and what You wanted to be out is out."

As God said through Paul in 2 Timothy 3:16-17:

> "All scripture is given by inspiration of God, and is profitable for doctrine, for reproof, for correction, for instruction in righteousness: That the man of God may be perfect, throughly furnished unto all good works."

Another "talk" went along these lines:

"Father, I know people say You 'didn't part the Red Sea,' or You 'didn't create the earth in six days,' that 'Christ wasn't born of a virgin,' or come back from the dead or go back up into heaven.

But, Father, I have seen so many things in the occult, and I know You are so much more powerful than the Devil. If the Devil can do the things that I have seen in the occult, I know You can part the Red Sea, I know You can create the universe in six days. You have the power to do anything You said You did. I believe You over any man."

I had read it just two nights before, in Psalm 118:8-9:

> "It is better to trust in the LORD than to put confidence in man. It is better to trust in the LORD than to put confidence in princes."

I trusted the Lord, and trusting His Bible was just like trusting Him. It was good enough for me.

I loved my new life. For the first time my life was being built upon a sure foundation: faith in God and His words in my King James Bible.

A few short months later I would retire to my bedroom at my mom's house, get out my guitar and my "mule-choker," open to the Psalms and just make up music as I sang them back to my Lord.

I would sing, and cry, and the tears would make it hard to read the words. Then I would wipe away the tears, start playing again, and the same thing happened, again and again and again. I was so happy that I was saved —and I knew it.

One day I heard that a friend of my brother was moving away. I asked him if he had a Bible, and he said no. And so I made a choice. I ran home and got my mule-choker and gave it to him. I gave it to my brother's friend, never to see it again.

Shortly after he moved away, I regretted letting go of that Bible. It took me almost 30 years to find another like it. But praise God, after years of searching, He let me get not just one, but two identical, first printing copies of the exact same Bible.

I try to keep one of them within eyeshot at home. It's sort of a reminder of how simple faith can conquer even the most complex of arguments. After all, it's faith that God wanted from us in the first place:

Hebrews 11:6 says:

> "But without faith it is impossible to please him: for he that cometh to God must believe that he is, and that he is a rewarder of them that diligently seek him."

Sometimes I think I was just plain smarter back then, with my King James Bible and a few Chick tracts, than I was in all the years of Bible college, Bible translation training and seminary, and then all the years of researching, all to find myself back where I had started 20 years before.

I was pulled away from the King James Bible by a well-meaning Christian the first time. But when I came back, it was to stay.

Don't be fooled into thinking that the Devil wouldn't use your closest friends and associates, pastors, teachers or family, to pry your hands off of that King James Bible. The battle has gotten fierce.

And I think Satan has gotten the idea that the time is almost ripe for his End Game: one world religion. Of course, it will only work if he can whittle down to one world Bible for that one world religion.

And let's not kid ourselves: he's almost there. There's just one last bastion that keeps holding him back and ruining his plans and spoiling his day: faith in the words God promised to preserve.

For English speakers, that force is faith in the King James Bible, God's preserved words in English.

Those who don't believe in God's preserved words, no matter what else they may believe and do, are basically pushovers, as far as the Devil is concerned.

But it won't stop there.

Satan has the world at his fingertips. As it is written in 1 John 5:19: "...the whole world lieth in wickedness."

It's time that God's people stood in faith against the wiles of the Devil, and perhaps, with God's help, held back the End for one more generation.

40

It "Reveals" the Most Changed New Testament Book

On the day of my wedding, June 20, 1987, my mentor and friend Dr. Mont W. Smith had a conversation with my future father-in-law. And believe it or not, we have photographs of that very conversation!

Dad said to Mont, "Sometimes I think David's gonna be too liberal."

And Mont replied, "Oh, no. Sometimes I think David will become too conservative!"

Who do you think was right?

One day, Mont and I were having a conversation about Creation vs. Evolution. We were talking about his brother, who believed that God took apes and evolved them into humans.

During that conversation Mont said to me, "David, if you take the Bible text exactly as it is written, you'll never be far off from the truth."

Mont was right, but which Bible? There are two! And there are incredible differences between them. One encourages faith; and the other, doubt. One lifts up Christ; one lowers Christ.

Let me give you an example from the Book of Revelation. I was witnessing to a Jehovah's Witness one day in front of the apartment, and I wanted to show him where Jesus says to the apostle John, "I am the Alpha and the Omega, the first and the last."

So I got out my New American Standard, opened it to Revelation 1:11, and there it ... ***wasn't!*** I quickly looked for another verse on a similar topic.

In that crucial moment I'd lost the opportunity to show this precious Jehovah's Witness, from a clear scripture, that Jesus Christ is God.

Do you think maybe the Devil wanted it that way? Do you think maybe he whispered to that Alexandrian scholar, "That doesn't belong in there! That must be some sort of mistake. You don't believe Jesus Christ is eternal God anyway, do you?"

And that Alexandrian scholar thought, "Hmm, that must be some kind of mistake." [Erase, erase, erase]

And in the ***very book*** that has such condemnation for the person who ***dares*** to add to or "take away from the words of the book of this prophecy," [Revelation 22:18-19] the book of Revelation became ***the most changed book in the New Testament***. Compared to the preserved words of God, the Alexandrian version of Revelation changes hundreds of places.

And did you know... in The New King James, those footnotes that say "M," pretending to be from the majority of texts (which they're not), actually changed the Book of Revelation over 600 times!

I'd rather have the King James Bible that lifts Jesus Christ so high.

It's not a matter of "liberal" vs. "conservative." Brothers and sisters, it's a matter of truth, God's truth, vs. the Devil's lies, no matter what form they take.

Choose wisely.

41

One Greek Letter Can Change the Gospel

Can just one Greek letter change the gospel from God-centered to man-centered? You are about to find out, in something as subtle as the announcement of Christ's birth by the angels in the Judaean hills, in Luke 2.

Believe it or not, that single letter changes the gospel.

Did God demonstrate "good will" toward man? Or did God only give "peace" to special "men of good will"? Which stream of manuscripts your Bible comes from makes all the difference.

Look at Luke 2:14 in the reading preserved through history by believing Christians from the Antiochian, northern stream of Bibles. You can find it in your King James Bible.

Luke 2:14: "Glory to God in the highest, and on earth peace, good will toward men." The key word here is εὐδοκία (*eudokia*). It is written in the "nominative" case.

That means it's the subject of a sentence or clause. So, it is saying that "good will" goes "toward men," obviously from God.

This shows that everyone is potentially included in God's good will. God's peace was made available to everyone through giving His only begotten Son.

"For God so loved the world that he gave..." (John 3:16)

He loved us so much that He "is not willing that any should perish" but is willing "that all should come to repentance." (2 Peter 3:9)

He wants us to have the only opportunity for true "peace" —peace between God and each one of us.

This made it possible for Him to be just, and yet completely wash away all our sins. And then He could adopt us as His own children through faith. It's as simple as "Ask and it shall be given you." (Luke 11:9-13)

Of course, multitudes will refuse to trust in God's sacrifice and be rightly judged, condemned for their sin on the judgment day. But that does not change the fact that offering His only begotten Son was a demonstration of God's will for peace "toward" all men.

He came as a good will gesture to all men. Jesus did not come just to offer peace to those who deserved it.

But guess what? When we follow the polluted Alexandrian, southern stream of manuscripts, the scripture is changed to just that!

The Alexandrian so-called "scholars" decided to add just one letter. It is called a "final sigma". It's a ς (S) at the end of that one word, *eudokia*. That changes the meaning from "nominative" case to "genitive" case. One way to think of it is like making a prepositional phrase, adding the word "of."

So the Alexandrian text says this: "Peace among men of good will."

There are a few ways of translating that. You could say those exact words, like the Catholic Douay-Rheims, the Noyes, or the Rotherham.

Or you could say, "peace among men with whom he is well pleased," like the 1881 ERV and 1901 ASV of Westcott and

Hort, or the 1964 Bible in Basic English.

Or you could use the lighter "with whom he is pleased" of the ESV, NAS, the Updated New American Standard, NET Bible, NIrV, NLT and RSV.

You could even say, "on whom his favor rests," like the Catholic New American Bible, NIV (1984 and 2011), Catholic New Jerusalem Bible, NRSV and TNIV.

But wait. I thought that "all have sinned, and come short of the glory of God" (Romans 3:23). Then how could some be "men of good will?" Even worse, how could anyone say he or she is someone with whom God is "well pleased?"

Think about those words! The only one God ever said that about is Jesus, at His baptism and at the mount of transfiguration. Is that saying that there are people on earth who are better than Moses and Elijah, and just as good as Jesus?

Do you see the problems this one letter creates? And yet, it is reflected in almost every single modern and Catholic translation in the world.

"Yes," you may say, "but does any of that actually affect anyone? It's just a single sentence from a Bible." Yes, it does. I can testify of that, because it happened to me!

From this starting point, we were taught in Bible college about man's good will, we were taught against the doctrine of "Original Sin," and the "fact" that people sin, but are not born away from God. It literally changed the entire doctrine of sin.

As a result of this and other verses, I actually spent time working on a re-translation of Paul's Epistle to the Romans. I was changing words related to "righteousness"(δικαιοσύνη, *dikaiosunē*) and God accounting us righteous, to God merely "acquitting" us of crimes we had committed.

This doctrine made me think that we weren't sinners in need of a Saviour. We were just overall "good" people who did bad stuff and needed to be forgiven of it.

This is completely wrong. But I worked on this while I was training to be a Bible translator!

What kind of translation would I have made? You know the answer: a man-centered Bible, not a God-centered one. And I testify to you that the one factor that led to this in my own life was a single "final sigma" –that one little Greek "S".

It would have given me lots of agreement from the unsaved, who think that something they do will gain them favor from God to save them.

The Roman Catholic hopes the sacraments will do it. Mormons hope they can keep "the laws and ordinances of the Gospel," which means a lifetime of obedience to their authorities.

Muslims hope that it comes from washings (wudu), prayers, pilgrimage to Mecca, and by some, waging Jihad. Even agnostics and atheists say, "I am a good person."

But God says, "No, you are not." Without God's grace and sending His Son Jesus to be the perfect sacrifice for our sins, we are without hope! And the moment you add a work to "grace," a gift, it is no longer a gift.

Romans 11:6 says:

> "And if by grace, then is it no more of works: otherwise grace is no more grace. But if it be of works, then is it no more grace: otherwise work is no more work."

By the way, the Alexandrian Bibles didn't just stop by adding that final "S". That southern stream even removed the last sentence of Romans 11:6 you just read, to hide the fact that works stop grace from being grace. Yes, brothers and sisters, it is that serious. Once you start changing the scripture, where do you stop?

This is why we need one Bible, God's preserved words in our language. These changes are subtle, tiny, almost unnoticed. But they cause a chain reaction that can literally change the gospel from one of grace by God, to one of works and worthiness of man —in a word, Humanism.

Choose carefully from which stream you drink.

42

Was Jesus God on Earth? NIVs Don't Seem to Think So

A sister in the Lord had a question the other day about the **Incarnation** (Christ becoming a human being). It's also called "**theophany**," God manifesting as a man. It ultimately boiled down to how and when the Lord Jesus Christ was both God and man.

It's an excellent question. I asked her to grab her King James and her NIV. Modern Bibles remove four important words that clarify an entire doctrine about Jesus being God and man.

Look at John 3:12-13:

> "If I have told you earthly things, and ye believe not, how shall ye believe, if I tell you of heavenly things? And no man hath ascended up to heaven, but he that came down from heaven, even the Son of man **which is in heaven.**"

Jesus was at that very moment talking with Nicodemus, who came to Him by night for fear of the Jews. He was also in heaven at that very moment. Twenty-seven modern Bibles completely removed those four words. Four modern Bibles rewrote them, so Jesus was God in heaven, but isn't now.

This was the <u>first</u> verse that I had in mind to show her. And if you look in 31 modern Bibles, including ALL NIV-types: NIrV, TNIV, NIV 84 and NIV 2011, the doctrine is **GONE**.

But there is a <u>second</u> verse I like to use. In the King James it shows that Jesus Christ was God, who *added on* the form of a human body. Philippians 2:5-9:

> "Let this mind be in you, which was also in Christ Jesus: Who, being in the form of God, thought it not robbery to be equal with God: But made himself of no reputation, and took upon him the form of a servant, and was made in the likeness of men: And being found in fashion as a man, he humbled himself, and became obedient unto death, even the death of the cross. Wherefore God also hath highly exalted him, and given him a name which is above every name:"

In verse 6, Jesus' position in the Godhead is not something He stole. He took nothing from the Father or the Holy Ghost. The Son has His own position, His own part in the Godhead. The Son is the One who added something to himself. He added the form of a human being.

In verse 7, the Lord didn't come with fanfare. He didn't come with trumpets sounding. He didn't invite the major media. In fact, He told people who had no major reputation the most important news of all: GOD has come to the earth to be born!

Let me stop there and compare it to the NIV. The NIV, 1984 and 2011, the NIrV and TNIV. all say the same thing: "he made himself ***nothing***." Only the NIV does this, mind you.

But in the King James, only ***His reputation*** is removed.

Jesus added humanity. So you know, the Tyndale, Geneva and Bishops Bibles also say "He made Himself of no reputation." This was by no means a new idea.

Making himself ***nothing***, however, was a very new idea, thanks to the NIV. In the King James, Jesus adds on to Himself, He does not take away. That's why it says, in verse 7, "… and ***took upon him*** the ***form*** of a servant, and was ***made*** in the ***likeness*** of men:"

Jesus took on a distinct human form, and took on flesh, as well. This makes perfect sense out of John 1:14:

> "And ***the Word*** was ***made flesh***, and ***dwelt among us***, (and we beheld his glory, the glory as of the only begotten of the Father,) full of grace and truth."

Christ ***adding*** to Himself is also why it says in Phil. 2:8 "And being ***found in fashion as a man***, he humbled himself, and became obedient unto death, even the death of the cross." Jesus not only humbled Himself to add on a human body, with all its physical limitations, He also humbled Himself and obeyed His Father, to the point of paying for all of our sins by dying on the cross.

So, because God's Son took on a body and humbled Himself to the point of death on a cross, verse 9 says: "Wherefore God also hath highly exalted him, and given him a name which is above every name:"

God couldn't make His son "more God," obviously. But His "Name," His "reputation," couldn't be higher. And not because of ***who*** Jesus is, but because of ***what He had done***. Because God the Father's Son bore the shame and humiliation of death on a cross, God gave Him a Name which is above every name.

Philippians 2:10-11:

> "That at ***the name of Jesus*** every knee should bow, of things in heaven, and things in earth, and things under the earth; And that every tongue should confess that ***Jesus Christ is Lord***, to the glory of God the Father."

How awesome this is! So it makes perfect sense that Jesus said, when He paid for our sins on the cross, John 19:30: "It is finished: and he bowed his head, and gave up the ghost." Jesus was DONE.

I could go into a thousand things, but we've got to move on. While Jesus was on earth, He was also in heaven (See also John 3:13.) Of course, an Alexandrian Gnostic, who doesn't believe that God would become a man, ***would remove those words***, just like the NIV and 26 other Bibles did, copying the Sinaiticus and Vaticanus and other Alexandrian texts influenced by Gnosticism.

If God the Son "made Himself nothing," then the only nature He'd have would be human, right? So, let me ask you, would this kind of a ***de-God-ized*** Son of God then have to live on earth as a *mere man*? To pay for sins, would He have to go to suffer in hell?

Jesus said, "It is finished," just before He died on the cross. Was that a lie? Was there *more* that Jesus had to pay? Before I answer that, let me show you another verse that the NIV has gutted of its meaning, because it trusted in the fake 1840 Sinaiticus and 1475-suddenly-appearing Vaticanus.

That's 1 Timothy 3:16: "And without controversy great is the mystery of godliness: ***God was manifest in the flesh…***" It doesn't get clearer than that. But Sinaiticus and Vaticanus lie and only say "Who was manifest in the flesh."

The gutsy NIV says, "He appeared in a body." I appeared in a body, too. So did you. That's a non-statement. There's no new information there.

But get this: Each time I tried to show my friend how Jesus was the God-man, God become flesh, at each point the NIV tried to stop me. Had I only looked in those verses in the NIV, *I would have found NOTHING about Christ's being GOD on earth.*

It doesn't matter if I could cobble together other verses, to make the case that Jesus was God. What about John 9:35? "Dost thou believe on the Son of God?" **Not in the NIV.** It copies Sinaiticus and Vaticanus instead: "Do you believe in the son of MAN?" Son of Man and Son of God are completely different. You worship the Son of God. You don't worship someone because he's the son of man. Ezekiel was called "son of man." Nobody would think of worshiping him!

At least the Sinaiticus was consistent. It also took out "Lord, I believe, and he worshiped Him." You're not supposed to believe in **man**. You believe in **God**. So no ifs, ands, or buts: the NIV *does* and *did* destroy the doctrine of Jesus as God and Man at the same time, in these verses.

And these are the very verses I would use to help my friend. But could Christians actually have that doctrine, of a Son of God with the God-part taken out? *Yes.* I have a 1975 book called ***Destined for the Throne***, by Paul E. Billheimer.

Let me show you a few tiny snippets from his book, starting about page 84:

> "The Father turned Him over, not only to the agony and death of Calvary, but to the satanic torturers of His pure spirit as part of the just desert (sic) of the sin of all the race. As long as Christ was 'the

essence of sin,' he was *at Satan's mercy* in that place of torment where all finally impenitent sinners are imprisoned upon leaving this life…

"While Christ was identified with sin, Satan and the hosts of hell ruled over Him as over any lost sinner. During that seemingly endless age in the nether abyss of death, Satan did with Him as he would, and all hell was 'in carnival.' This is part of what Jesus bore for us."

According to this and many other passages, where it says over and over, things like this:

"As long as He was identified with sin, He was in the clutches of Satan and the hosts of hell, *just like any lost sinner*."

And then finally this:

"Thus, in order to be made alive unto God and restored to fellowship with His Father, *He* [Jesus] *had to be reborn.*"

So, there is a doctrine that Jesus died as a human. When Jesus said, "It is finished," it was a lie. Not only was it *not* finished, *it had just begun*. According to this doctrine, the Father not only let devils torture the Lord Jesus for three days and three nights, The Father Himself also poured His divine wrath on His Son. And Jesus had to take it, that is, until He was reborn —born again. But Philippians 2, which the book never mentions, says that because Jesus paid the price for us *on the cross*, God highly exalted His name.

Billheimer's book says Jesus *couldn't* have paid for sins that way, and instead He had to be tortured by devils and have all the wrath of God the Father poured out on Him. That is heresy. Can you believe that?

But, if you have a Bible like the NIV, changing verses about how Christ was both God and man, I can see how it happened.

I read the endorsements of this book. There's a really big one by Paul Crouch, formerly of TBN, saying how it was the 2nd most important book of his and Jan's life, next to the Bible.

Then there's a foreword. I found this interesting. It doesn't mention the stuff about Jesus, but it is still a ringing endorsement:

> "I have ... been inspired and challenged by the insights and **fresh *interpretations of the Scriptures*** ... Every Christian who feels impelled to find a ***deeper dimension of Christian witness*** should not only **read** this book, but ***study it prayerfully***, and ***apply its principles to his life***. —Billy Graham

When I read and trust my King James, I get a clear idea of what God said about His Son, and how He was God and man at the same time. But from modern Bibles like the NIV, I find emptiness.

That's probably why there's such a crisis of faith in even believing in the simple doctrines of Jesus. I'm sticking to my clear, understandable King James Bible.

43

It Helps You Ask the Right Questions

People have written in saying they're surprised by the attitude I have, which is different from what they'd expect in a King James Bible believer. I can sum it up in three words: Always ask questions.

And I have some questions for you. When I was in Bible college, my professors told me that only the Original Manuscripts, the Original Autographs, were inspired of God.

So a question came up: Then where *are* the "Original Manuscripts"? "Oh, they don't exist anymore," they would say.

Which brings up another question: "You only have faith in the Originals that don't exist? Where did you come up with this idea that only the Originals were inspired?"

And if they answer: "Well, from the Bible..." then I'll say: "But how do I know if I can trust your Bible, since you don't believe in anything but the Original Manuscripts, and you don't have them?"

It's circular reasoning, you see? God never said only the original manuscripts were inspired, in any manuscript, in any language —anywhere!

What *did* God say? In Deuteronomy 4:2 God said:

"Ye shall not add unto the word which I command you, neither shall ye diminish ought from it, that ye may keep the commandments of the LORD your God which I command you."

And God said through Solomon, in Proverbs 30:5-6:

"Every word of God is pure: he is a shield unto them that put their trust in him. Add thou not unto his words, lest he reprove thee, and thou be found a liar."

How can you know whether you've added to or taken from God's words, unless you have them, a standard by which you can check?

Here's another question. After recording Jesus' temptation in Luke 4, Jesus came into Nazareth. Luke records that He read from a scroll, which turns out to be Isaiah 61:1 to the beginning of verse 2.

What did Jesus call that copy of a copy of a copy that He held in His hand? Luke 4:21: "And he began to say unto them, This day is this **scripture** fulfilled in your ears."

My professor says it's *not* scripture. Jesus says it *is* scripture. I don't know about you, but I trust Jesus, God the Son. It's scripture!

Scripture is the word given by God to define the words that are given by inspiration. Are you with me so far?

Okay.

Now God promised in Psalm 12:6-7:

"The words of the LORD are pure words: as silver tried in a furnace of earth, purified seven times. Thou shalt keep them, O LORD, thou shalt *preserve* them from this generation for ever."

Do you know that these words are so threatening that

modern publishers have rewritten them in their Bibles?

But they couldn't rewrite what Jesus said in Matthew 24, Mark 13 and Luke 21: "Heaven and earth shall pass away, but my words shall not pass away."

It's God's responsibility —and promise— to preserve His words.

I'm saved by grace through faith. I trust that God gave us John 3:16. I'm saved by its words. I also trust God's promise to preserve His words.

Years of study have shown that God's preserved words are exactly where I'd expect to find them: with His faithful people, often at the price of their lives.

Does your church have a statement of faith that says they only believe in the Original Autographs? If so, where did they get it from? It's nowhere in my Bible!

So next time somebody comes up to you and says, "I only believe the Original Autographs are God's inspired words," then you can say, "Tell you what: You show me the inspired Autographs that you put complete faith in, and I'll show you the preserved Bible that I put complete faith in."

44

It's Nothing to be Ashamed Of

Many of my friends have heard me talk about my mule chokin' King James Bible. And some of you, who have listened to the videos, have heard that reference. What is that?

Well, I foolishly gave it away to somebody about a year or so after I had returned to the Lord, instead of recommending he go buy his own.

It took me 30 years to find an exact replica, still wrapped in plastic, in the original box! Does this make me a fanatic? Well, maybe it does.

You have baseball fanatics —baseball "fan," right? But let me ask you: When you go walking around, do you have a little Bible that you hide underneath menus or napkins? When I came out of the occultic stuff that I had been into in 1980, after August 24th to be specific, I burned all my occultic stuff.

And all my friends at Palms Springs High School know that I carried my occultic stuff right where everybody could see it. So it was nothing different for me, when the only thing I knew that had the word of God was THIS Bible, that I carried it around.

I wasn't trying to thump people over the head with it. I wasn't trying to be mean, or anything. I just believed it! So I carried it with me because I believed it and I wanted to read what it said, and I wanted to learn. And that's when I started reading through the whole Bible from Genesis and from Matthew simultaneously for the first time.

Later I was given a New American Standard, and it went downhill from there. But by the time I did go to Fuller Seminary I had read through a Bible 3 times, because at least I believed "the Bible," whatever it was.

But when I had the big KJV, I had no problem carrying such a big book around, because I believed it was true.

Romans 1:16 is not there by accident. It says:

> "For I am not ashamed of the gospel of Christ: for it is the power of God unto salvation to every one that believeth; to the Jew first, and also to the Greek."

And in Luke 9:26 our Lord Jesus Christ spoke to His disciples:

> "For whosoever shall be ashamed of me and of my words, of him shall the Son of man be ashamed, when he shall come in his own glory, and in his Father's, and of the holy angels."

I don't want Jesus to be ashamed of me. I cannot be ashamed of His words. So even if this is the Bible I'm carrying when you see me, then there you go.

I've got my mule chokin' King James Bible, not because I'm hitting people over the head, but because I truly believe it. If you don't have a Bible you believe, get rid of the Bible you have and get yourself a King James Bible.

I believe every word of this Book. I may not understand every word, but I believe it. And I am not ashamed of it, no matter what size Bible I carry.

45

It Makes It Easy to Share Your Faith

Last Sunday a preacher in our area talked about his favorite sports hobby. He was so excited! Someone saw him and complimented him on it. Then he and the pastor had a short conversation about the sport, though not about Christ or salvation.

Anyway, this pastor gladly told the congregation all about it. Then he dropped all the enthusiasm as he went back into the main sermon topic.

One brother in Christ said to me, "I wish I could see him as enthusiastic about spreading the gospel as he is about that sport."

In fact, the few times I saw him hold up a tract over the years, it was accompanied by the statement that he didn't hand it to an unsaved person, but rather, to another Christian, in case he wanted to give it out.

He had such enthusiasm for his favorite sport, but couldn't even hand out a single gospel tract, much less speak the gospel message to someone outside church.

Is it any wonder why his large congregation doesn't evangelize, either?

There are 10 verses that say "preach the gospel," referring to Christians. But in pulpits, Bible colleges and seminaries, the Great Commission has become the Great Omission.

Why did this happen? And what can you and I do about it?

Jesus gave the Great Commission at the beginning of His 40 days of post-resurrection appearances to His disciples, on a mountain in Galilee. That's Matthew 28:16-20.

Jesus also gave the Great Commission to His disciples toward the end of the 40 days, before He ascended to heaven. That's Mark 16:15 and following.

Jesus even commanded the disciples to be witnesses, in the last moments before He ascended into heaven on the 40th day, as it says in Acts 1:2-10. So why do people treat the command to "Share our faith" as if Jesus commanded us to "Pull our own teeth"?

One reason people don't actively share their Christian faith is the Bible they use.

It makes a difference when a person reads John 7:8 only to find that his or her Bible says Jesus was a liar to His brothers.

It makes a difference when people's Bibles take away "without a cause" in Matthew 5:22, making Jesus a sinner because He was angry when He cleansed the temple —twice.

It makes a difference when there's a note in the Bible in the only two Gospel passages that say Jesus ascended to heaven, Mark 16:19 and Luke 24:51, which says they are not in the Sinaiticus and thus not in the so-called "oldest and best Bible." Suddenly, they realize that their Bibles say Jesus may not have ascended into heaven, just like professors have been teaching in colleges and seminaries for years.

It makes a difference when they say that salvation is based on faith, but their Bible says it is "difficult" in Matthew 7:14 and "hard to enter into the kingdom of God" in Mark 10:24. The fact that other verses say the opposite doesn't help.

Now their supposedly "holy" Bible —contradicts itself!

And why? Because it depends upon the Codex Sinaiticus, first, and Codex Vaticanus, second. So, their Bible changes the text to match those corrupt Bibles.

No wonder they don't share their faith. They're not even sure what it is! What is it today? Will a new papyrus throw out another belief?

But many Christians who read and believe the King James Bible are active sharers of the gospel. They have one Bible that they trust. They believe their own Bible. Imagine that!

And because they have one consistent message from Genesis to Revelation, they can say "Thus saith the Lord" quoting the inspired writings of the apostles and prophets, and have no fear of being wrong.

That is a person who can know his or her faith. And that is a person who will want others to have that faith, too.

Remember: every single religion in the whole world says that you have to do good works, enough good works, to balance out your bad works to let you experience heaven or Nirvana or paradise or whatever.

Only Bible-believing Christianity teaches that the works for salvation were done by Jesus Christ Himself. And what He commands us to do is admit our sinfulness, our need of Him, and believe what He did, shedding His precious blood to pay for all our sins.

Only Bible-believing Christianity says it's a relationship that gets us into heaven, not a religion. So, no man can have that kind of fake power over us.

When you place your trust in Christ, and His blood pays for your sins, you are forgiven, become a new creature and get adopted by God the Father! That's it! You're saved!

In that relationship, we have the opportunity to grow and

gain rewards by obeying our heavenly Father. Salvation is not a reward. And only saved people get rewards.

Christ gave one command over and over again and repeated it through His apostles: Preach the gospel; be His witnesses.

That's why Chick Publications exists. That's why I'm here. I want a way to place a basic gospel message into a story. When people are drawn in and read the story, they also are told that basic gospel message.

I spend so much time talking about what the real Bible is, because I want people to realize how trustworthy God is, to read and believe their Bibles, and be so encouraged by its message that they have to share it!

The day I received a Chick tract as a 9-year-old, I went to my next door neighbor, a girl named Debbie (no relation to my wife), and led her through the tract.

And I asked if she wanted to receive Jesus as her Saviour, as that man had just asked me less than an hour before! And she said yes! And we prayed!

And in 1998, only about two days after I came to trust that God preserved His words in English in the King James Bible, I kindly faced a Jehovah's Witness and his son in my front yard. And my simple going through the scriptures was so threatening, the Jehovah's Witnesses suddenly emptied the street of all women and children and did a Jericho march around my property! And not even their "expert" wanted to talk with me.

I cried out, as they marched away, "I just don't want you to go to hell!" Where did that boldness come from? I was convicted of the truth, and I could no longer sit idly by while people around me went to hell.

If you want others to be brought to the point where they

hear the gospel and can choose Christ, Chick tracts are for you —or rather, for you to give to them.

If you want to know why you can trust your King James Bible, and why you don't need to be afraid of the inconsistent, doubting Bibles, I have books and videos on the subject. Chick Publications is here for you, too.

That's why Chick Publications exists: to help people spread the gospel in this busy, hectic world that desperately needs Jesus. But to do that, you have to be confident in your Bible!

I hope this inspires you. I just started putting a variety of tracts in my pockets, because so many people around me have already seen the newest ones. Praise God!

Truly, if you don't get to see the results in this life, you will definitely see your rewards and the souls you reached in heaven.

Maybe next time that pastor will use the opportunity to hand out a gospel tract.

46

It Doesn't Need Updating

Did Ezra make a youth Bible when he had a chance? Why or why not?

It was a day of celebration. An amazing event had taken place. After 70 years of captivity, the children and children's children had returned to Jerusalem, to their ancestral home.

Nehemiah, their temporary governor, had faced many obstacles with them to get them to this point. There were Sanballat and Tobiah, political and religious enemies.

There were false prophets and prophetesses, false brethren and false accusations. Tobiah and his son even married into Jewish families, to try and sneak in and mess up God's people.

And despite the looming threat of extinction by Israel's adversaries, the Lord had caused the wall of Jerusalem to be built around the city in just 52 days! What a feat!

Now the people were resettled in their cities and it was time for the Feast of Tabernacles, for Ezra the priest to read to them out of a copy of the Law of Moses to the people —all 50,000 of them.

There was just one problem.

A lot of people didn't understand the Hebrew terms anymore. What's a priest to do? This was a classic opportunity to "update" the Bible.

There were terms the young people did not know. There were concepts the next generation had never been taught. And who knows? The parents may have even come up to Ezra and said, "Remember, Ezra —you don't want to lose the young people!"

Ezra could have made "cultural substitutes"—that is, he could have taken elements of Babylonian culture and put them in to substitute for the old Bible words.

He could have made an RBV, Revised Babylonian Version, Youth Edition. It was a perfect opportunity. It was classic!

But did he? Not a chance!

Ezra did what God commissioned him, as a priest and his people, the Levites, to do: he arranged to teach the people.

The priests and the Levites circulated among the people, helping them to understand God's words —but they read every word of what God had said, to them.

They didn't change a word!

Take a look for yourself in Nehemiah 8:8:

> "So they read in the book in the law of God distinctly, and gave the sense, and caused them to understand the reading."

That's what God has called us as Christians to do.

The Lord Jesus Christ, in Matthew 28:19-20 said:

> "Go ye therefore, and teach all nations, baptizing them in the name of the Father, and of the Son, and of the Holy Ghost: Teaching them to observe all things whatsoever I have commanded you: and, lo, I am with you alway, even unto the end of the world. Amen."

Teach them. Then when they're saved, teach them some more.

We cannot compromise God's words with "cultural equivalents" and pass that off as scripture.

I trust these examples from the scriptures: I will read my Bible, God's words, the King James Bible, God's preserved words in English, and I will gladly help them "to understand the reading."

That way they'll be lifted up, to understand God's words, instead of (dare I say it?) dumbing-down the holy scripture of God. That way we can observe to do all things that Christ has commanded us, without compromising. And Christ will be with us.

I hope you will join me in not dumbing-down —I mean, updating— the words of God.

47

KJV Vocabulary Is Easier Than You Think

Is King James English too hard to understand? I've got a fun little test for you. See if you can fill in the blanks.

Here is a song. See if you can fill in the blanks in your mind.

"My country ____ of _____, sweet land of liberty, of _____ I sing."

Did you get it? Here's another one.

"America, America, God _____ His grace on _____, And crown _____ good with brotherhood from sea to shining sea."

Here's another one. This is the 6th Commandment. "_____ _____ not kill."

Jesus said, "____ _____ love _____ neighbour as _____."

Do you know what the words are?

Jesus said, "For _____ is the kingdom, and the power, and the glory, for ever. _____."

Juliet said, "__ Romeo, Romeo! _____ _____ _____ Romeo?"

How about this song? You modern people might know it. "_____, __ Lord, _____ a shield about me..."

Lincoln said, "Four _____ and seven years ago our fathers brought _____ on this continent a new nation..."

Have you got it?

Jesus said, "Judge not, _____ _____ be judged."

She says the King James is too difficult?

"_____ the lady_____ protest too much!"

Look at all the vocabulary I just gave you!

I gave you 16 words. Here's my list: 'tis, thee, shed, thy, thou, shalt, thyself, thine, Amen, O, wherefore, art, score, forth, lest, and ye.

I threw in methinks, but actually 2 Samuel 18:27 has "Me thinketh" so that's pretty close.

There are only about 600 "archaic" words in the King James Bible and you already got 16 of them.

How hard can this be? I have great confidence in your ability to understand the Bible.

Have fun. Learn the words and realize once you know an archaic word, it isn't archaic anymore...especially when you start to believe it —and use it.

48

What Publishers Are Hiding

I'm happy to see that Bible publishers are coming out with new printings of the King James Bible and King James study Bibles, King James reference Bibles, and then with the higher prices on leather, they're also coming out with leather substitutes that hold together pretty well.

But there's a secret that these publishers are hiding.

Those new study Bibles have anti-KJV, Bible-doubting footnotes! Why? Because these publishers don't believe the King James Bible is God's preserved words in English, and they don't want you to believe it, either!

Why? Because if you did believe that the King James Bible is God's preserved words, then they wouldn't make a lot of money from you. You wouldn't be buying all their alternate versions and alternate editions.

You see, when I got the NIV Bible handed out to me for free, in Bible college, the first thing I wanted to do, and did, is get an NIV Greek-English New Testament, an NIV Hebrew-English Old Testament, and a NIV concordance, and NIV dictionaries, and Bible handbooks and references.

But a couple of years later, guess what happens? A new version comes out! And it's got new endorsements from your favorite ministers, it's now required in Bible college, your preacher is preaching from it, it's the preferred Bible that's put up on your screen at church, and wow!

That's a *lot* of extra sales! But there's something you need to know. ***These big Bible companies are not owned by Bible-believers.*** Zondervan is under HarperCollins, under News Corporation, under Rupert Murdoch. In 2003, World Bible Publishers was bought by Thomas Nelson. In 2012, Thomas Nelson was bought by secular HarperCollins, under News Corporation, under Rupert Murdoch. That adds up to 55% of the Bibles.

I can stop right there. You see, someone could say, "David, seriously, why are you picking on these Bible publishers? They don't actually write these books." But see, a publisher decides what will be published. If they don't like the material that's in it, they will not publish it. End of story.

There's a lot of business to be had, getting people to doubt the word of God.

> "For the love of money is the root of all evil: which while some coveted after, they have erred from the faith, and pierced themselves through with many sorrows." (1 Timothy 6:10)

> "For we are not as many, which corrupt the word of God: but as of sincerity, but as of God, in the sight of God speak we in Christ." (2 Corinthians 2:17)

See, there's a sinister motive in getting people to doubt God's preserved words. It's so they can make money off us with all these Bibles and Bible materials. Don't let them manipulate you into spending all your hard-earned money on faith-destroying Bibles, footnotes and materials. Get yourself a King James Bible of good quality (without the doubting footnotes) and put your trust in God's words. Trust me. It will pay off in the end.

49

What About My Congregation?

A brother in Christ who is a pastor wrote to me about a change that has happened in his life. He has come to believe that the King James Bible is God's preserved words! But what about his congregation? How can this pastor gently lead them to the truth?

Want to know what I told him?

This pastor went to Bible college and seminary and learned textual criticism and worked with Greek texts, much like I did. Bible college required the New American Standard. Seminary lifted up both the New American Standard and the English Standard (ESV). The church where he started preaching largely used the NIV. And the church where he'd spent years preaching now, was hooked on the Holman Christian Standard. People were even given free copies of it after their baptism.

Here is his problem. Only one or two people in his church use the King James. As a whole, he's got this congregation full of the Holman Christian Standard, and he wants to lead them to the King James Bible.

I love how he put it: "Perhaps I better understand the phrase, 'I believe, help thou mine unbelief!'"

The pastor wrote, "I want this to be a time when the people I am honored to lead are reassured of their faith and the confidence they can have in the Word of God, rather than a time of confusion and doubt. I am sure there will be those who disagree, but that comes with any change. I am just looking for help."

So I prayed. Then I wrote this back to him: "This is basically what I would say, were I addressing your congregation. I leave all the amenities to you. I just wanted you to have the basic approach, as I believe it is both godly and right, and a way of peace, as well.

"This isn't a matter of bashing other versions. It's a matter of saying, and being able to say, 'Look! I finally trust what God said, because I am confident I actually have what God said, not man's opinions.'

"I'm not telling you what you can and cannot do. Everybody in Christ is a person in transition. We are transitioning from saved sinner to growing saint, from unholy to holy, from righteous solely by the decree of God to righteous in lifestyle, from God working salvation in us to taking that salvation which is our own, and working it out in our daily lives.

"Like it says in Philippians 2:12-13, '...work out your own salvation with fear and trembling. For it is God which worketh in you both to will and to do of his good pleasure.' Because we are in transition, we continually reevaluate what is better, and what is best.

"If you want to know why I've stopped jumping around from version to version, it's because I finally believe I have God's words in English. I don't have to go looking anymore. I've found them. My job now is to believe them and to obey them, whether I fully understand them or not.

"If you had just found a treasure map in your field, but it

was in language you sometimes found confusing (and treasure maps aren't always clear), what would you do? Wouldn't you first sit down and take the time to understand every word, so you would be sure to find that treasure, that you have just found out is on *your* property?

"The same is true with God's holy words, the Bible. When you know you have what God said, you don't want to run to something else. You won't be satisfied with someone's guesses and interpretations turned into something called a 'translation.' You will want only what it actually says because God's words *are* the treasure. God's promises are attached to His words! That is why we must know that we *have* God's words, in order to have confidence in His promises!

"I now have that confidence. I hope you will, too. But please understand, from now on I will consult many people's opinions, but I will only have **one authority**, and believe it. For me now it is plain. I trust that the King James Bible is God's preserved words —holy and preserved— in English.

"I am willing to spend the time, for the rest of my life, learning the truth about the treasure I now hold in my hands. I hope you will have that confidence and find that confidence that I have, in this book, too."

50

You Can Be Just Like the 90% — Or…

Do you think my belief in the King James Bible has gone too far? Do you think I've "gone overboard" in saying it is God's preserved words in English? What I'm about to say may surprise you.

You don't have to accept my arguments. You don't have to believe what I say. You can be just like the 90% of Bible-owners in the world.

Of course, that also means you will get what they get. You get to have a Bible (there are a lot of Catholic-approved Bibles to choose from) that leads you to doubt basic doctrines.

You get to have a Bible with contradictory Bible verses. You get to have a Bible that has a "Jesus" that sinned because He got angry —at least three times. You get to have doubts about which words, phrases, and verses really belong in your Bible. You get to have doubts about the doctrines that are contained in those words, phrases, and verses.

You get to try to have a consistent Christian life, and maybe even witness to others. But of what? About an inconsistent god who can't even get His own book right? About a de-powered god who isn't big enough to make sure He keeps His own promises to preserve His own words?

If He can't take care of His own book, how can He take care of your soul? If that's the kind of god you worship, be my guest. Just please understand if I refrain from worshiping that god. My God makes promises. My God keeps promises. My God, in history, kept His promises to preserve His words, in English, faithfully, through history, in what we have as the King James Bible, tested over 400 years.

So, read your paraphrase, read your watered-down dynamic-equivalence Bible, read your comfortable King James look-alike. But I am going to stand on what God promised and preserved. In English, the King James Bible.

I don't just read these words. I believe them. I don't leave home without them. And *know* I'll be prepared for heaven with them.

51

Just One More Question

It's amazing. You show a person 50 reasons why you trust the King James Bible, and he says, "Well, can you answer one more niggling question? 'Cause if you can't, I'm just gonna have to stick to my version."

This well-meaning person has put the cart before the horse. Believe it or not, you don't need to answer that question right now.

What you need to do is get their eyes back on the Big Picture.

The Devil simply loves to get our eyes off of what is really important and onto what is less important. That is why we use up our time trying to find out the secrets of the universe, when the Main Point is sitting right in front of us.

What IS the Main Point? The Main Point is this: Everything that matters in the Christian life is based upon FAITH. The Devil will do everything and anything in his power to distract us to something we cannot answer at the moment, and confuse us, to get us to DOUBT God and His words.

The Devil is systematic. It's the same tried-and-true method, all the way back to the Garden of Eden. The same four steps we covered in chapter 21:

1. Confusion - Yea, hath God said? Did God really say that?
2. Doubt - I'm starting to doubt that God actually said that.
3. Disbelief - I don't believe that God really said that.
4. Rebellion - I don't have to do what that says.

God answers so many of our questions, but He does it in the proper order. First we settle the Big Picture. Then we can work on the tiny questions. Otherwise, we will be, as it says in 2 Timothy 3:7, "Ever learning, and never able to come to the knowledge of the truth."

So how do we turn it around? Ask them a few questions yourself:

1. Do you believe God?
2. Do you believe what God said?
3. Do you believe God's promise to preserve His words?
4. If so, then you ask them this question: "Where are God's promised, preserved words?"
5. What kind of people does God say that He will use, according to the scriptures?

2 Chronicles 16:9, He wants a people whose heart is perfect toward Him.

2 Timothy 3:12 says, "Yea, and all that will live godly in Christ Jesus shall suffer persecution."

So, you look for people who are persecuted for their godliness. Look for the kind of people God says He wants to

Just One More Question

work with and find out what kind of Bible they trust.

In English, the question's already been settled: the King James Bible. Over 400 years strong, tested and reliable.

That's good enough for me. I trust the scripture, God's words in English, the King James Bible, even if I don't have all the questions of the universe settled yet.

But what about those niggling questions? Do we just give up on them? No. Let's be patient. Relax. Just because we don't know the answer, doesn't mean there isn't one.

Remember Shadrach, Meshach, and Abednego?

> "If it be so, our God whom we serve is able to deliver us from the burning fiery furnace, and he will deliver us out of thine hand, O king. ***But if not***, be it known unto thee, O king, that we will not serve thy gods, nor worship the golden image which thou hast set up." (Daniel 3:17-18)

These are people of faith. They didn't know that God would deliver them. But they still trusted that He could, and they acted in faith.

Faith, not doubt, is what God is looking for. That's why it is the basis of our relationship with Him. Hebrews 11:6 says: "But without faith it is impossible to please him: for he that cometh to God must believe that he is, and that he is a rewarder of them that diligently seek him."

Appendix:
Getting Bible Facts Straight

There are 790,868 words, total, in the King James Bible. There are 12,843 unique words in the King James Bible, and a total number of 31,102 verses. That's a lot of verses.

That's an even number so that means there is no exact center. You divide it into two equal halves and verse 15,551 and verse 15,552 are the center verses of the Bible.

That's Psalm 103:1-2. Here are those words:

> "Bless the LORD, O my soul: and all that is within me, bless his holy name. Bless the LORD, O my soul, and forget not all his benefits:"

Those are awesome words. But that's not all of it. There's also 1,189 chapters to the Bible. So that means there are 594 chapters before Psalm 117, and 594 chapters after Psalm 117.

So, when you're going through your Bible, you will notice that one chapter sits alone, Psalm 117. Right? Not 118. How many verses are in Psalm 117? Two.

You have 2 center verses as well, when you try to do it by chapters. When you go to the chapters you have Psalm 117 in the middle. But Psalm 117 is just 2 verses, so it's an even number again, so it's verses 1 and 2. All of Psalm 117 is the center of the KJV Bible by chapters:

> Verse 1: "O praise the LORD, all ye nations: praise him, all ye people.
>
> Verse 2: For his merciful kindness is great toward us: and the truth of the LORD endureth for ever. Praise ye the LORD."

Appendix Getting Bible Facts Straight

Here's a couple more of our facts: Psalm 117 is also the shortest Psalm of the Bible, with only 2 verses.

And the middle verse of the New Testament is Acts 11:17, where Peter says:

> "Forasmuch then as God gave them the like gift as he did unto us, (talking about Cornelius and the gang at his house) who believed on the Lord Jesus Christ; what was I, that I could withstand God?"

These are just a few Bible facts that I thought I'd share with you. The next time someone tells you "The middle verse of the Bible is Psalm 118:8," You say, "No, it's not." And you just show them for yourself. Psalm 117 is the center by chapters. And Psalm 103:1-2 is the center by verses.

I spent the time on this because I trust the King James Bible. Isn't it wonderful, that in a world where new versions (and new editions) come out in a never-ending stream, there is one Bible that we can trust, which is worth taking the time to count even its words, chapters, and verses?

King James Bible Facts At-a-Glance

Entire Bible

Chapters: 1,189
Words: 790,868
Verses: 31,102

Center Verses: Psalm 103:1-2
Center Chapter: Psalm 117
Center Verses of Center Chapter: Psalm 117:1-2

New Testament

Center Verse: Acts 11:17

ALSO BY DAVID W. DANIELS

256 pages, paperback

Before you buy another Bible, look at what's being left out!

- See how one left-out word makes Jesus a liar in 19 modern Bibles!
- See which entire verse was removed to leave room for infant baptism.
- See the verses where adultery is removed from God's sin list.
- Does your Bible warn of hell? Many don't!

ALSO BY DAVID W. DANIELS

288 pages, paperback

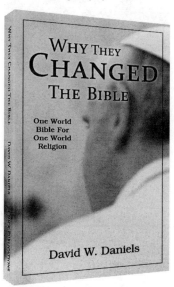

Bible translators, all over the world, are making Bibles that they think are only for Protestant and Baptist believers. But most don't know that Christian translators are being manipulated into helping create a One-World Bible! And all the translation work is paid for by contributions from Bible believers like you. **Who** is behind this? And what do they believe?
Read, as they admit it, **in their own words!**

ALSO BY DAVID W. DANIELS

112 pages, paperback

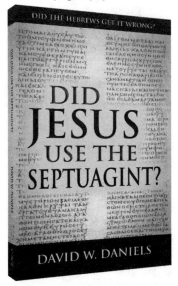

That's what they may have taught your pastor in college. Do you know why?

Simple: the Septuagint contains the Apocrypha, and there are people who want your pastor (and you) to have the Apocrypha in *your* Bible, too. Why? So you will accept Catholic superstitions like:

- Purgatory and prayers for the dead
- Payment to forgive sins
- Angels as mediators

In this new book, David Daniels takes each of the "proofs" promoting a BC Septuagint and shows why they can't be trusted. He shows that Jesus read the same Hebrew Scriptures as other devout Jews. Don't be fooled by the push for "One World Bible for One World Religion".

ALSO BY DAVID W. DANIELS

208 pages, paperback

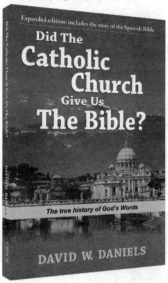

Expanded edition includes history of Spanish Bible.

The Bible has two histories. One is of God preserving His words through His people. The other is of the devil using Roman Catholic "scholars" to pervert God's words and give us corrupt modern Bibles.

Read the history of not one, but two Bibles... One that matches centuries of evidence, and another that has been changed to justify Catholic doctrine.

ALSO BY DAVID W. DANIELS

160 pages, paperback

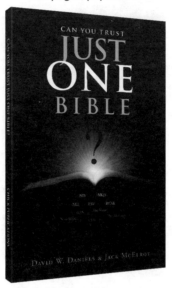

by David W. Daniels & Jack McElroy
Do we need multiple Bible translations?
Or is there one Bible we can simply trust?

Christian leaders tell us we need to compare several, to get as close to the "lost originals" as possible. But that just breeds doubt.

In early 2015, authors Jack McElroy and David W. Daniels recorded two unrehearsed interviews where they answered many anti-KJV accusations. The videos are on YouTube, but this print version has much MORE information.

ALSO BY DAVID W. DANIELS

224 pages, paperback

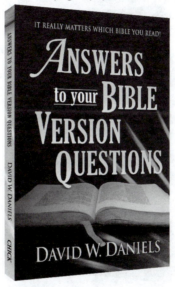

Did God preserve His words?
Or does my Bible contain errors?

If you believe God preserved His words, where can you find them?

History shows that there are two streams of Bible texts, and they are not the same. Obviously, both of them cannot be correct.

Respected linguist David Daniels proves beyond a doubt how we can know the King James Bible is God's preserved words in English. He answers many of the difficult questions the so-called "experts" throw against the King James.

Whether you want to defend the King James Bible or learn which Bible you can trust, you will find the answers here.

ALSO BY DAVID W. DANIELS

352 pages, paperback

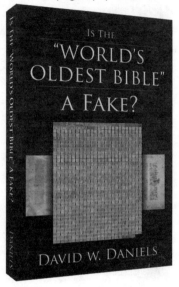

Publishers are making significant changes to match an "old" Bible called the "Sinaiticus." In this new book, David W. Daniels proves the Sinaiticus is a 19th century hoax with easy-to-understand evidence.

Why are they doing it? To change the Bible text to one that can accept everyone's doctrine, to be One World Bible for One World Church.

NOTES

NOTES